THE ART STUDENT'S GUIDE

TO

EXTERNAL ANATOMY

EDITED AND DESIGNED BY TOM RICHARDSON

2

Published by Tom Richardson
ISBN 978-0-9821678-5-4

INTRODUCTION

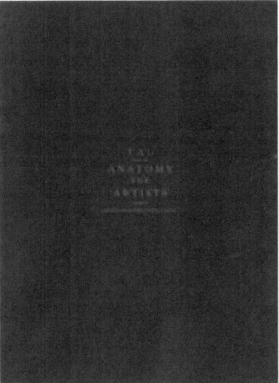

This book is one of two that are based on the pioneering anatomical plates for art students first published by Doctor Julien Fau. They have similar plates from two sources. This full color edition titled ***The Art Student's guide to the External Forms of Man*** is a republished edition of the color plates from ***The Anatomy of the External Forms of Man, Intended f or the Use of Artists, Painters and Sculptors*** by Doctor J. Fau, Lithographed by M. Leveille, pupil of M. Jacob, New edition with additional plates by William Norris published originally 1849. The book was published in 2 parts, one the plates, the second a treatise on the plates for the purpose of studying the external anatomy of man for artists. The text of the book was translated into English by Robert Knox, M.D., Lecturer on Anatomy, and corresponding member of the National Academy of Medicine of France.

The other edition is titled ***The Art Student's Guide to Anatomy in Art*** which reproduces the black and white engravings does not include that translated text, but rather a text written by Jonathon Scott Hartley in 1891 which combines an easy to understand description of the appearance and actions of the bones and muscles, with a concise description of the plates and has additional chapters on sculpting, muscles of the deeper layers, and human proportion.

The plates in two versions are different. The first book reproduces the full color stipple engraved plates from ***The Anatomy of the External Forms of Man, Intended for the Use of Artists, Painters and Sculptors*** the second reproduces the black and white engraved plates from ***Anatomy in Art*** by Jonathon Scott Hartley. Both books have their origin in the French works by Dr. Julien Fau.

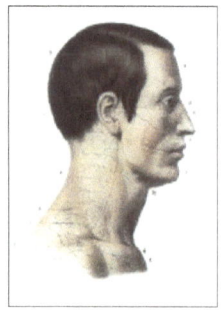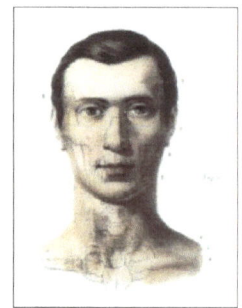

The following information about Dr. Fau, the editor of the book is from Ludwig Choulant's *History and Bibliography of Anatomic Illustration*, published in 1920.

JULIEN FAU

Julien Fau, doctor of medicine in Paris, edited two different anatomic works for artists: **Anatomie des formes exterieures du corps humain, a l'usage des peintres et des sculpteurs. Avec un Atlas de 24 planches dessinées d'apres nature et lithographiees** par M. Leveille, eleve de M. Jacob. Paris: Mequignon-Marvis fils, 1845 (16 and 214 pp.), 8° and fol. (24 lithographic plates), black and white and also colored.

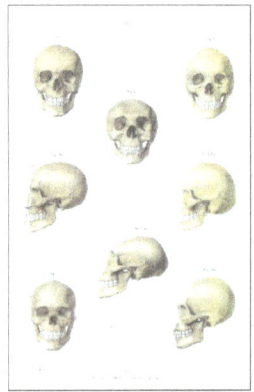

The plates are very beautifully finished and comprise one plate of skulls of different nationalities; several different views of the nude bodies of a man, a woman, and a child, all drawn from nature, some of them supplemented by skeletons placed alongside of the bodies, with the body outlines; representations of the bones, and the muscles, the latter with the bones in some cases drawn in.

Particular attention has been given to the various positions and flexions of the extremities. The last plate represents the myology of the Laocoon, without the sons, after Charles Clement Bervic's well-known print. This work has been translated into English, with additions, by the physician Robert Knox, and published under the title: **The anatomy of the external forms of man, intended for the use of artists, painters and sculptors**, London, 1848, with an atlas of 26 plates in quarto; published in black and white and also colored.

The second, smaller, and less expensive work by Fau is: **Anatomie artistique elementaire. Dessins d'apres nature** par J. B. Leveille, gravures sur acier. Paris: Mequignon-Marvis, 1850, 8°, with 17 steel engravings in 8°, three of which are in small folio. In this work the representation of the shapes of skulls, of the nude bodies, and of the Laocoon are missing, but representations of three beautiful skeletons, with the contours drawn around them, have been added. The remainder deals with osteology and myology, although less exhaustively than in the previous work.

Both Dr. Fau's original descriptive text and Robert Knox' English translation are available on the internet at Google Books. Robert Knox published his own book **Artistic Anatomy for the use of Sculptors, Painter, Amateurs** in 1852. This book included many illustrations and serves as a summation of the knowledge of anatomy of the time. You can read a copy on the internet at Google Books.
Fau begins his preface:

> Il n'est personne aujour d'hui qui conteste l'ulilité del'anatomie artistique. L'homme éclairé ne néglige aucun moyen d'augmenter ses connaissances : le savant, l'artiste consciencieux, ne méprisent aucun renseignement ; doués d'un esprit observateur, ils discernent tout d'abord ce qui peut leur être utile, le reste s'efface de leur souvenir.

This is the beginning of Robert Knox's translation of Julien Fau's preface.

AUTHOR'S PREFACE.

No one disputes at present the utility of a knowledge of Anatomy to the Artist. The enlightened man neglects no means of extending his knowledge; the skilful, the conscientious Artist, despises no education; gifted with a spirit of observation, he discerns at once what is likely to prove of benefit to him ; the rest escapes his memory.

Artists have occasionally ridiculed Anatomy as an Art of no utility to them; a feeling which seems due to an exaggerated independence of spirit. How could such minds stoop to learn Anatomy, who despise the instruction, nay, the very influence of a Master, trusting wholly to their own imagination? Enlightened men, avoid such troublesome errors of an overheated imagination.

Artists may rest assured that Science never presumed to govern or regulate the Fine Arts; its efforts are confined to the offering them, in a friendly way, some knowledge likely to be useful to them,—some, of an incontestable utility. I do not hesitate affirming, that of all the studies to which Artists ought to devote their attention, the most important is the study of the External Forms of Man. In support of this assertion, I may cite that of great Artists (Painters) who not only caused their students to attend anatomical lectures, but themselves wrote anatomical works, or drew anatomical plates. Albert Durer, Leonardo da Vinci, whose work was illustrated by Poussin; Jean Cousin; these unquestionably are no mean authorities.

There are two modes of studying Forms:—1st, the servile imitation of the model:—2nd, the anatomical study of the human body.

The first, entirely mechanical, leaves in the mind of the student feeble impressions only, quickly effaced or modified; the second, based on observation and reasoning, produces a lasting impression, resisting the caprices of the imagination. It is not enough that an Artist is competent to copy exactly an academy figure ; this is merely a work of manoeuvre, of handicraft; he must ascend to causes, discover for himself the origin of the Forms he is called on to reproduce; in a word, he must know how to decompose in order to recompose; then only will he become competent to reproduce the work of Nature; directed by genius and judgment, he will not overstep the limits of Truth.

Of the two methods just alluded to, the one produces Painters, the other Artists. I do not pretend to say that the study of Anatomy is sufficient to make an Artist; I take it for granted that the student is irresistibly drawn towards this profession, to which we owe Michael Angelo, Raphael, Benvenuto-Cellini, &c. A person is not necessarily an Artist inasmuch as he cultivates the Fine Arts.

But it must be admitted, that if the Anatomy of Forms be not more generally attended to, the fault or omission rests not wholly with the student.

A Professor (Lecturer on Anatomy) imagines himself teaching Artistic Anatomy, when in truth he has merely been describing the bones and muscles to his audience, without ever directing their attention to the results of their arrangements; and when, at the end of the course, the student has copied one or two e'corchees (dissected figures, bodies) he fancies that he thoroughly understands the Anatomy of Forms, and that he has completed his anatomical studies! Fatal confidence, the sad results of which quickly show themselves in his works.

Should the Artist be desirous of studying that science profoundly, taught its utility even by its superficial study, and consequently alive to the insufficiency of the knowledge so acquired, what now does he find? Some collections of plates, almost always inexact, though decorated with the title of "the Anatomy of Artists;" a few fragments scattered through some laboured scientific works, overlaid by the weight of their envelope. To place in the hands of the student plates without a text, is to offer to the workman an instrument without the necessary instruction as to its use; and yet it were almost better to do so, than refer him to those lucubrations, extremely learned, no doubt, but of little utility to him, and always out of place in elementary works.

The works of Artistic Anatomy (Pictorial Anatomy) hitherto published, have in reality influenced the Fine Arts but little. At the very moment when the empire of Form was at its height, these works were rejected, a copying of the mere models being preferred by Artists, because, in such works, nothing was found but an inexact reproduction of the cadaveric dissections. The Gladiator, of Salvage, is conceived in a happier spirit; it is a more conscientious work; but unfortunately it is not a Treatise on Forms being merely an application of this science to one of the finest works of antiquity. The two plates of Martinez ought also to be mentioned, not on account of their exactness, but with reference to the thought or conception which gave rise to them.

The origins of continental Europe's acceptance of the science of evolution and the resistance to the theory in the United States may be deduced from the contrasts evidenced in the difference between the matter of fact manner that Dr. Fau begins his chapters titled ARTISTIQUE DU CORPS HUMAIN - GÉNÉRALITÉS and the way Robert Knox begins his, here is Dr. Fau:

L'anatomie est une science qui a pour but l'étude de la structure et de la forme des êtres organisés. Appliquée aux arts du dessin on la désigne sous le nom *d'anatomie plastique* ou *des formes;* elle est différente de *l'anatomie médicale,* en ce que celle-ci étudie des régions qui, comme]es n erfs et les viscères, ne contribuent pas aux formes extérieures et ne sauraient avoir pour l'artiste aucune application.

La partie fondamentale de toute recherche d'anatomie artistique, c'est la connaissance du squelette dont l'étude constitue ce qu'on nomme *l'ostèologie;*elle est importante parce que les os renseignent sur les proportions, les formes, les mouvements:

Pour les *proportions:*car les os dans certaines régions sont situés immédiatement au-dessous de la peau; ils fournissent alors des points de repère invariables sur lesquels on peut prendre des mensurations (malléoles, rotule, pointe du coude, etc.);

Pour les *formes:* les régions que nous venons de signaler y contribuent dans une large part; on peut citer également la face interne du tibia qui est sous cutanée. Les os, donnant attache aux muscles, nous renseignent, par les points où ceux ci s'insèrent, sur l'emplacement occupé par les masses charnues;

My translation:

GENERAL CONSIDERATIONS ON MAN AND ON THE MODIFICATIONS HE UNDERGOES THROUGH MORAL AND PHYSICAL INFLUENCES TEMPERAMENTS, RACES.

Anatomy is a science that aims to study the structure and form of organic beings. Applied to the arts of design it is referred to as anatomy or plastic forms and is different from medical anatomy, in that it explores areas such as the nerves and organs do not contribute External forms and should not be the artist for any application.

The fundamental part of any search for artistic anatomy, is the knowledge of the skeleton whose study is what is called osteology and is important because the bones provide information on the proportions, shapes, movements: For proportions because the bones in certain regions are located immediately beneath the skin, they then provide benchmarks invariable which can take measurements (ankles, patella, elbow tip, etc.). For forms: the regions that we have just mentioned contribute to a large extent, one can also cite the medial tibia is subcutaneous. The bone, giving attachment to muscles, inform us, by those points where they fit on the site occupied by the fleshy masses;

This is how Robert Knox begins his translation:

The gift of an intelligence superior to that of all other animals leaves man nothing to envy them on the score of structure. Hence, I do not sympathize with those misanthropic philosophers, who have drawn a parallel between man and other animals in favour of the latter. According to them, the finest gifts of nature have been denied to man.The undulating forms, the slender, yet agile limbs, at times robust and of matchless strength; the gorgeous display of colours with which nature has decorated the animal kingdom; these, she has denied to the human species. In lieu of such qualities, unbefitting his kind, she has bestowed on him a superior intelligence, by means of which he overcomes all other animals, thus carrying out the great destinies of his race.

The admirable harmony of the human forms, cannot, for an instant, be mistaken or overlooked; man's position on the soil, his walk, his gesture, the expression of his countenance, pourtraying his sensations, feelings and intellectual energy; all are in harmony with his physical organization. The reverie of those who imagined man to have exhibited a quadruped form at first, altered into the biped by civilization alone, cannot be admitted even as a theory; it is a dream at variance with all anatomy and physiology.

From there he digresses into a a discussion of temperaments and races using Petrus Camper's discredited theories on facial angles.

Whatever the differences in the translated text in the various national editions, the plates and the descriptions of the plates remained the same and these books were widely circulated with almost every art student in possession of one or the other to advance his or her understanding of anatomy.

There were as many as ten editions of the book published in French, English, Dutch and German. The **Anatomie Artistique Elementaire** (referred to popularly at the time as *Petit Fau)* has shortened descriptions and only 17 steel engraved plates.

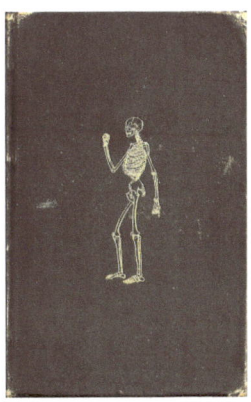

The American version by Jonathon Scott Hartley has additional illustrations and notes on sculpting, muscular anatomy and human proportion. This was a self published book which contains the same steel black ink engravings as *Anatomie Artistique Elementaire*. Hartley's book combines the plates with extensive commentary on anatomy and a chapter on proportion and the art of modeling (sculpting in clay).

The Nation (Vol. 53 No. 1382,December 24, 1891) printed the following brief review:

—Mr. Jonathan Scott Hartley, N.A., S.A.A., who was for many years the instructor in anatomy of the Art Students' League, has prepared from his lectures a small handbook for for art students called 'Anatomy in Art,' which may be had of the author, at No. 145 West Fifty-fifth Street. Such treatises on this subject as have hitherto been published have very generally had two faults: they have been written by surgeons rather than artists, and have been burdened by a mass of detail which is practically useless to the artist and only confusing to the student; and they have been too costly for the proverbially slim purses of art-students. This book is written by a professional sculptor of standing, who has omitted much useless and cumbering information, and confined himself to the description of those bones and muscles which affect the surface appearance and are, therefore, necessary to be known, and it is published at a reasonable price. We do not think the ideal book on anatomy for art-students has yet been written. In that book not only the descriptions but the plates should be confined to the few great fundamental truths of the figure. The plates should be rather diagrams than detailed drawings. Such a book is to be desired, but, in the meantime, Mr. Hartley's book is a step in the right direction, and we know of nothing better at present existing. The plates are reproduced from Fau's costly work, and are supplemented with drawings from Schadow's work on ' Proportion,' and with reproductions from photographs of the living model in action. Mr. Hartley has added a short treatise on " The Art of Modelling," which his great practical knowledge should make very useful to beginners.

The Photographic Journal of America, Wilson's Photographic Magazine, Vol. 27, 1890 has this biography of Jonathon Scott Hartley:

J. SCOTT HARTLEY

'The minds of all earnest photographers are now turned toward the Daguerre Memorial just unveiled in Washington, the gift of the American photographers in commemoration of the "Father of the At," so called. Naturally there is interest felt in the American who has been chosen as the artist of the occasion. All know that this honored person is Mr. J.Scott Hartley of our city. Some months ago Mr. H. McMicbael, of Buffalo, sent us a sketch of Mr. Hartley's career and a photo-engraving of him. We thought it best to reserve their publication until now.

J. Scott Hartley is a noted figure in American sculpture—an art which has taken its rise in this country within the last half century. H. K. Browne, recently deceased ; Greenough, of New York ; and E. D. Palmer, of Albany, were the pioneers.

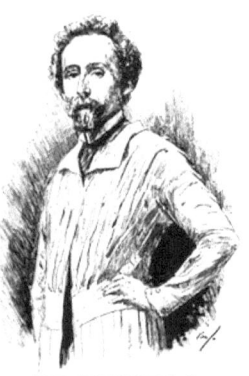

Mr. Hartley began his art career under Palmer, of Albany, about twenty-five years ago—a studio whence came some men of international prominence. Since then he has been prolific, variable in idea and illustration, and the number of his works, always bearing the signs of an individual genius, are remarkable.

Twenty years ago Mr. Hartley took a Royal Academy medal in London, and worked and studied in Germany, Italy, and France. When he returned to the United States it was to consort with the new and fresh schools of art without accepting any of its extravagancies, and thereby is the strength of this faithful artist.

He was largely concerned in the foundation and subsequent prosperity of the Art Students' League, and was, during the struggling period of this now important factor in the art of the country, twice President and its first Professor of Anatomy, a position which he held for seven years of appreciated service.

Mr. Hartley was the founder of the Salmagundi Club, now the most exclusive and influential body of artists on the Western Continent, where men of all specialties in art are welcome, but they must come with good work to pass through the stile.

Mr. Hartley's principal works are the statue of Miles Morgan, one of the Pilgrim Fathers, now standing in Springfield, Mass., a commission from H. F. Morgan, of New York; it is a robust figure, eight feet high, and is well known to all New Englanders: The Whirlwind, which gave him a high reputation in the realms of plastic art showing, as it did, not only a profound knowledge of anatomy, but a subtle treatment of the harmony of lines in drapery and beauty of form: also a number of reliefs in the Saratoga monument commemorative of the surrender of Burgoyne : a colossal bust of J. P. Howard, who built the present University of

Vermont: a recumbent figure representing the Defeat of Satan, which was awarded a gold medal at the American Art Association, 1887, by the artists.

But perhaps what has given Mr.Hartley his greatest fame is the bust of John Gilbert as Sir Peter Teazle made only a year ago, from life, and a month before the great comedian's death. Amongst his recent sitters have been Edwin Booth, Barrett, Felix Morris, John Ryle (the founder of the silk industries in this country), and that princess of finished actresses, Ada Reban.

Enumeration is not necessary in the multiform works of this man, who by acclaim in the art world of New York is at the top of his profession.

Mr. Hartley was honored by being elected a member of "the Players," some months ago, and he is an associate member of the National Academy of New York.

Another English edition with plates was Elementary Artistic Anatomy of the Human Body, Translated and edited by Charles Carter Blake was published in 1881. There is a reference to Carter Blake in Charles Darwin's letters, Blake was an advocate of the discredited study of cranioscopy, which tried to make sense out of the races by a study of skulls. There was a schism in Victorian science with some arguing that cranioscopy proved distinct races, and ethnologists arguing for the unity of the races.

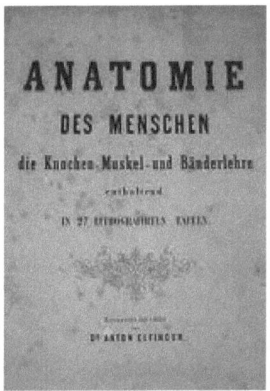

A German edition of Dr. Fau's book was published by Anton Elfinger (January 15, 1821 - January 19, 1864). His book titled *Anatomie des Menschen, die Knochen-Muskel- und Bänderlehre* enthaltend in 27 lithografirten Tafeln. Bevorwortet und erklärt von Dr. Anton Elfinger was published in 1854. It has 27 lithographs of which three seem to be original designs by Elfinger.

These also appear in *The Anatomy of the External Forms of Man, Intended for the Use of Artists, Painters and Sculptors* which is the basis for my republished edition. Anton Elfinger was a physician in Austria. He studied at the Academy of Fine Arts in Vienna under Leopold Kupelwieser and after his studies there took up the study of medicine, less by choice than at the urging of his family, earned his doctorate in 1845. He became a permanent employee of the Vienna General Theaters newspaper and contributed costume pictures which he signed "Cajetan." He also contributed illustrations to Humoristisch-Satiriscen Volkskalender and was a cartoonist and political cartoonist.

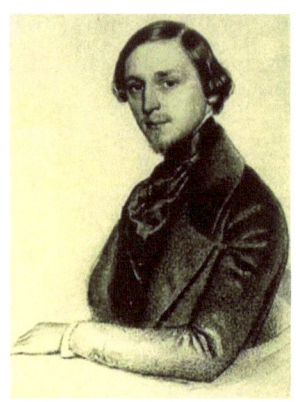

Dr. Elfinger worked with a dermatologist, Ferdinand von Hebra and was an illustrator of medical literature. He produced the watercolors for Hebra's Atlas der Hautkrankheiten (Atlas of Skin Diseases). Another book he illustrated is *Horizontaler Durchschnitt des Menschlichen Auges*, by Dr. Arlt published in 1875. This book illustrates the human eye.

A brief biography appeared in *Biographisches lexikon der hervorragenden aerzte aller zeiten und völker*, 1885. Here is a translation of the biography.

Biographical lexicon of the outstanding physicians of all times and peoples

Elfinger, Anton E., in Vienna, was born in 1822, where he was also doctor and was a practicing doctor and a draftsman. The greater glory of his credit is the unprecedented "Atlas skin diseases" by Ferd. Hebra (Vienna 1856 - 66, fol.), For a number of years at the General Hospital of Vienna he produced Watercolor Paintings of the most characteristic cases of skin diseases with astonishing fidelity the plates of which were then reproduced with equal fidelity in the State Publishing House. He also provided for the teaching of drawing: "*Anatomie des Menschen die Knochen - Muskel - und Bandelehre*" "Vienna, 2 Ed 1854, 27 Taff. Fol.). He also modeled in wax anatomical objects of great skill and has, under the pseudonym "Cajetan" a substantial amount of caricatures, Rebus and thousands of illustrations for newspapers, calendars and other documents drawn. He died in the prime of life on 19. January 1864.

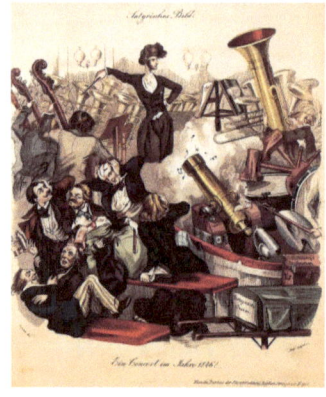 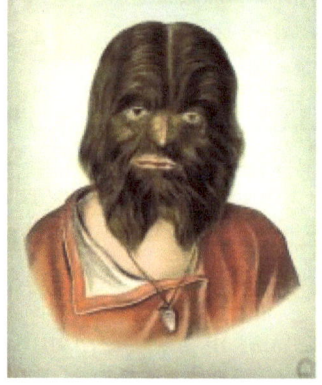

A book about Dr. Elfinger was published in 1966, *Cajetan. Das Leben des Wiener Mediziners und Karikaturisten Dr. Anton Elfinger* by Margarethe Poch-Kalous.

She says that after 1853 Dr. Elfinger may not have had steady employment as a medical illustrator and sculptor of anatomical parts which may be why he turned to illustrating for publication. She says he published "*Anatomie des Menschen die Knochen - Muskel - und Bandelehre*" on his own but points out in the footnotes that his contribution was three plates and an expanded introduction. The three plates are also reproduced in this English edition. They are Plate 6, the Female Figure - Side View, Plate 26, the Dissection of the Gladiator and Plate 27 the Dissection of Discobolus.

- Tom Richardson, 2010

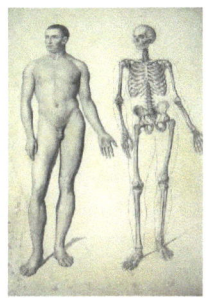 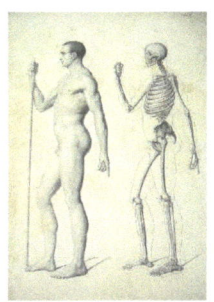 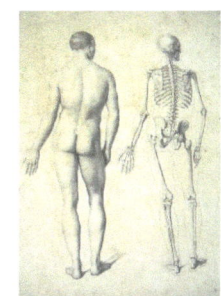

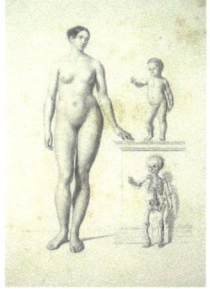 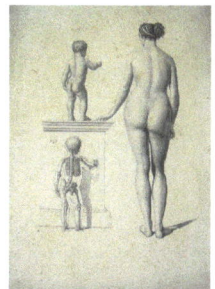

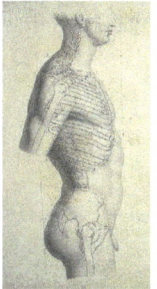 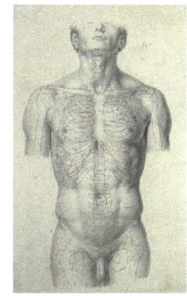 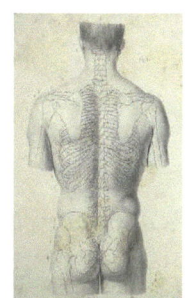

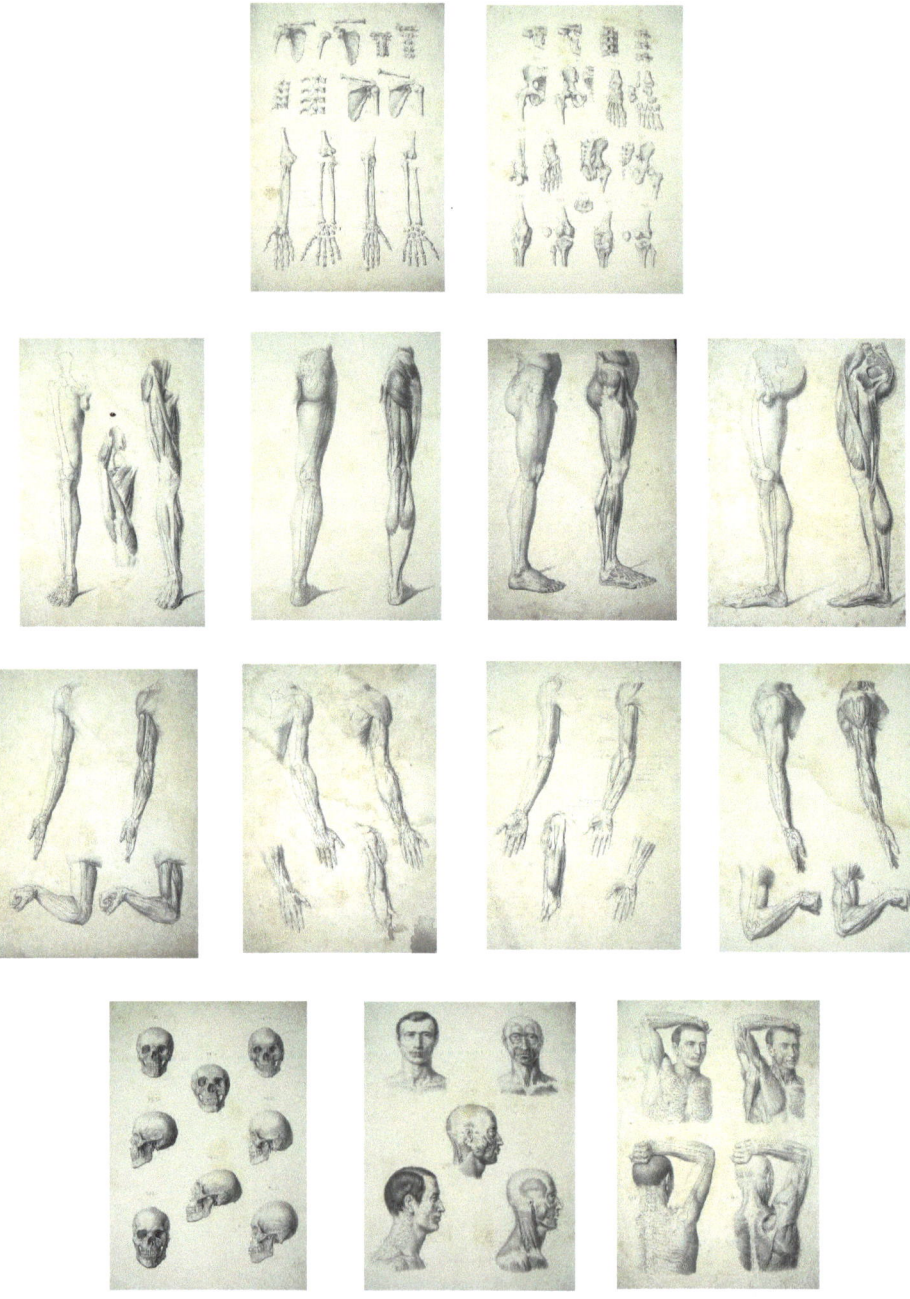

Photographs of plates from
Anatomie des Menschen die Knochen - Muskel - und Bandelehre
by Anton Elfinger

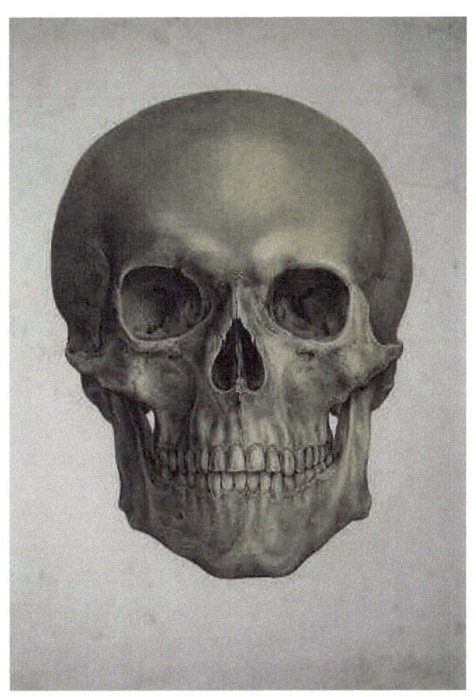

Plate of a skull from
Anatomie des Menschen die Knochen - Muskel - und Bandelehre
by Anton Elfinger

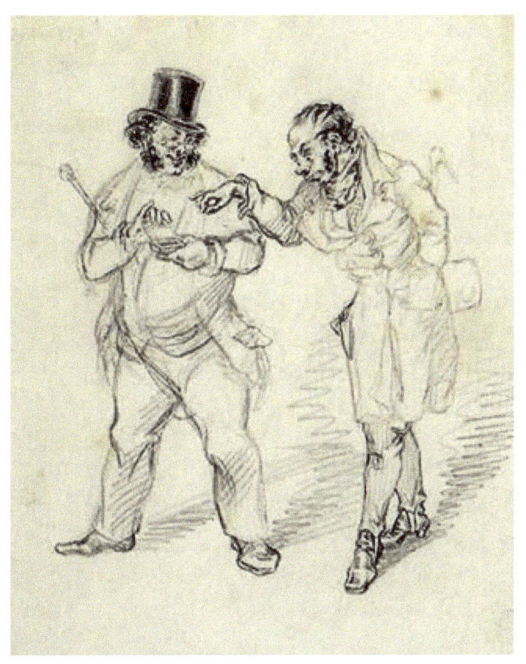

Eine Prise Schnupftabak *(A Pinch of Snuff)*
by Cajetan (Anton Elfinger)

Table of Contents

THE

ANATOMY

OF THE

EXTERNAL FORMS OF MAN,

INTENDED FOR THE USE OF

ARTISTS, PAINTERS, AND SCULPTORS.

BY DOCTOR FAU

———————————

ATLAS

Containing Twenty-Eight Drawings from Nature:

LITHOGRAPHED BY M. LEVEILLÉ, PUPIL OF M. JACOB

———————————

New Edition with additional Plates

BY WILLIAM NORRIS

ART MASTER AT THE NATIONAL ART TRAINING SCHOOLS, SOUTH KENSINGTON

THE

ANATOMY

OF THE

EXTERNAL FORMS OF MAN,

INTENDED FOR THE USE OF

ARTISTS, PAINTERS, AND SCULPTORS.

BY DOCTOR J. FAU.

ATLAS

Containing Twenty-Eight Drawings from Nature;

LITHOGRAPHED BY M. LEVEILLÉ, PUPIL OF M. JACOB.

New Edition with additional Plates.

BY WILLIAM NORRIS,

ART MASTER AT THE NATIONAL ART TRAINING SCHOOLS, SOUTH KENSINGTON.

LONDON:

BAILLIÈRE, TINDALL, & COX, 20 KING WILLIAM STREET, STRAND.

LECHERTIER, BARBE, & CO., 60 REGENT STREET, W.

PLATE I.

FIGURE 1.

1. Frontal bone.
2. Parietal bone.
3. Temporal bone.
4. Occipital bone.
5. Malar, or cheek bone.
6. Superior maxillary, or upper jaw bone.
7. Bones of the nose.
8. Inferior maxillary, or lower jaw bone.
9. Last cervical vertebra, or bone of the neck.
10. Clavicle, or collar bone.
11. Scapula, or shoulder blade.
12. Sternum, or breast bone.
13. First rib.
14. Seventh rib.
15. Twelfth rib.
16. Twelfth dorsal vertebra.
17. Fifth lumbar vertebra.
18. Sacrum.
19. Coccyx.
20. Iliac bone.
21. Humerus, or arm bone.
22. Cubit, or ulna.
23. Radius.
24. Carpus, or carpal bones; eight in number.
25. Metacarpus, or metacarpal bones; five in number.
26. Phalanges, or bones of the fingers; fourteen in number.
27. Femur.
28. Rotula.
29. Tibia.
30. Perone, or fibula.
31. Tarsus, or tarsal bones; seven in number.
32. Metatarsus, or metatarsal bones; five in number.
33. Phalanges of the toes; fourteen in number.

NOTES.

FIGURE 1.

In the engraving, No. 19, which should mark the coccyx, has been omitted; but the student may readily ascertain the situation of the coccygeal bones, which follow the sacrum as a direct continuation of the great column of the back. The figures 20 have been placed by the artist to mark what is here called the *iliac bone*. The term *coxal bone* would, perhaps, be more precise, for, properly speaking, there is no *iliac bone* in the adult. In this country, we call the large broad bone, forming either side of the pelvis, the "nameless bone" (*os innominatum*); in young persons it is formed of three separate bones, called iliac, ischial, and pubic. Moreover, the student must carefully remember whilst drawing this figure, and fixing its *proportions* in his mind, that he is occupied with the *male figure*. The finely formed *female* skeleton presents widely different proportions, as I shall afterwards more fully explain. British artists generally do not seem to be aware of this; I allude of course to the more finely formed skeleton, in the construction of which Nature has carried out the law of perfect formation, or of individuality to its utmost extent.

FIGURE 2.

This figure is intended to represent the whole of the forms, the outline, or *silhoutte* of the body, seen in front, and the proportions. The dotted lines, slightly traced at the top of the head, and under the heel, point out the direction of the line of gravitation.

PL.1.

Fig 2

Fig 1

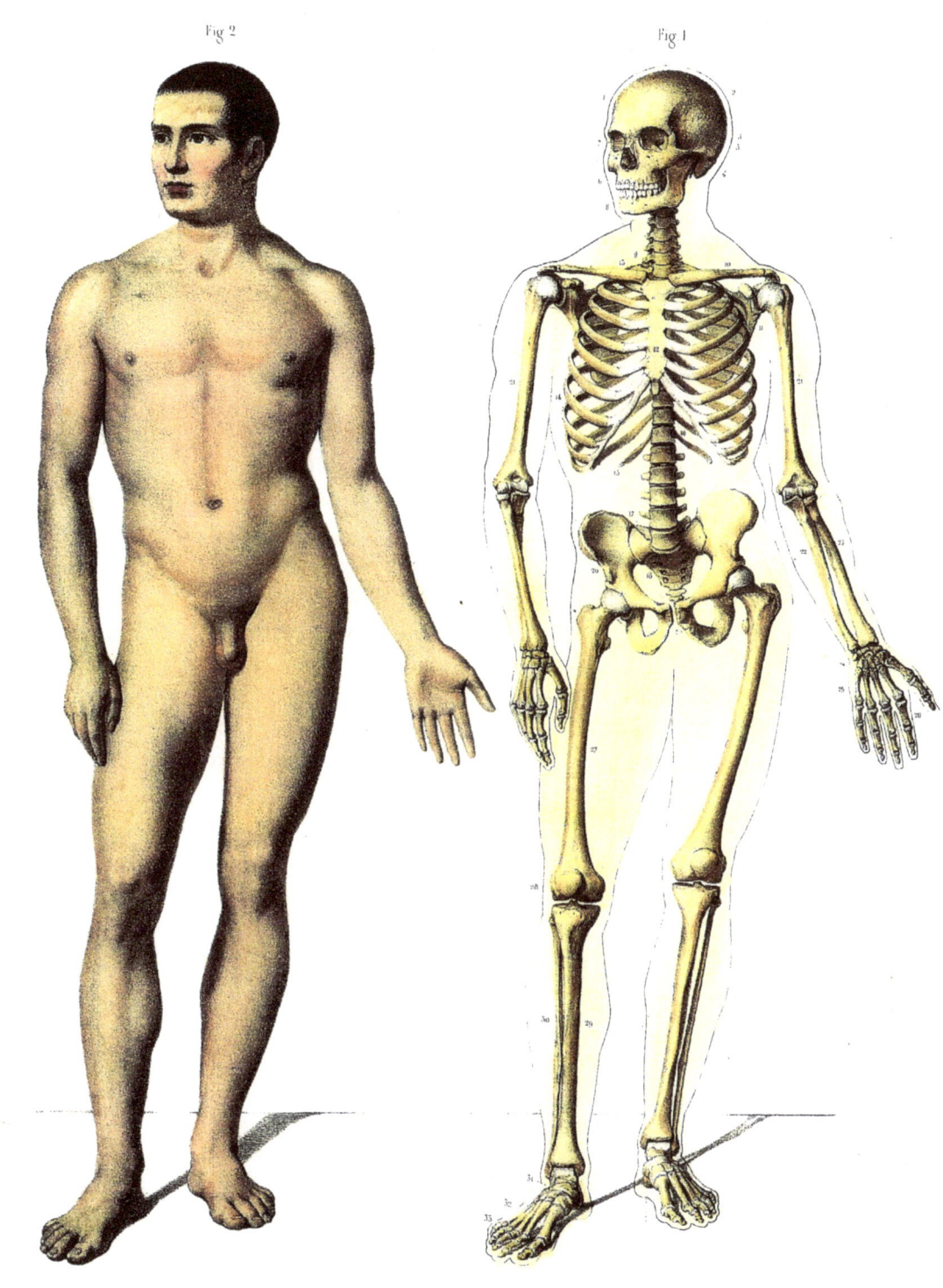

Fau 2.me édition.

Paris

Imp Lemercier,Paris

MÉQUIGNON MARVIS. GERMER BAILLIÈRE.

PLATE II.

FIGURE 1.

The whole body as viewed from behind.

FIGURE 2.

1. Parietal bone.
2. Occipital.
3. Temporal.
4. Malar.
5. Inferior maxillary.
6. First vertebra of the neck.
7. Seventh vertebra of the neck.
8. Twelfth vertebra of the back.
9. Fifth vertebra of the loins.
10. Sacrum.
11. Coccyx.
12. Coxal, or haunch bones.
13. First rib.
14. Last rib.
15. Collar bone.
16. Scapula.
17. Humerus.
18. Cubit.
19. Radius.
20. Carpus.
21. Metacarpus.
22. Phalanges.
23. Femur.
24. Tibia.
25. Fibula.
26. Tarsus.
27. Metatarsus.
28. Phalanges.

NOTE.

No. 10 in the Engraving should be placed higher up, and on the sacrum.

PL. 2

Fig 1   Fig 2

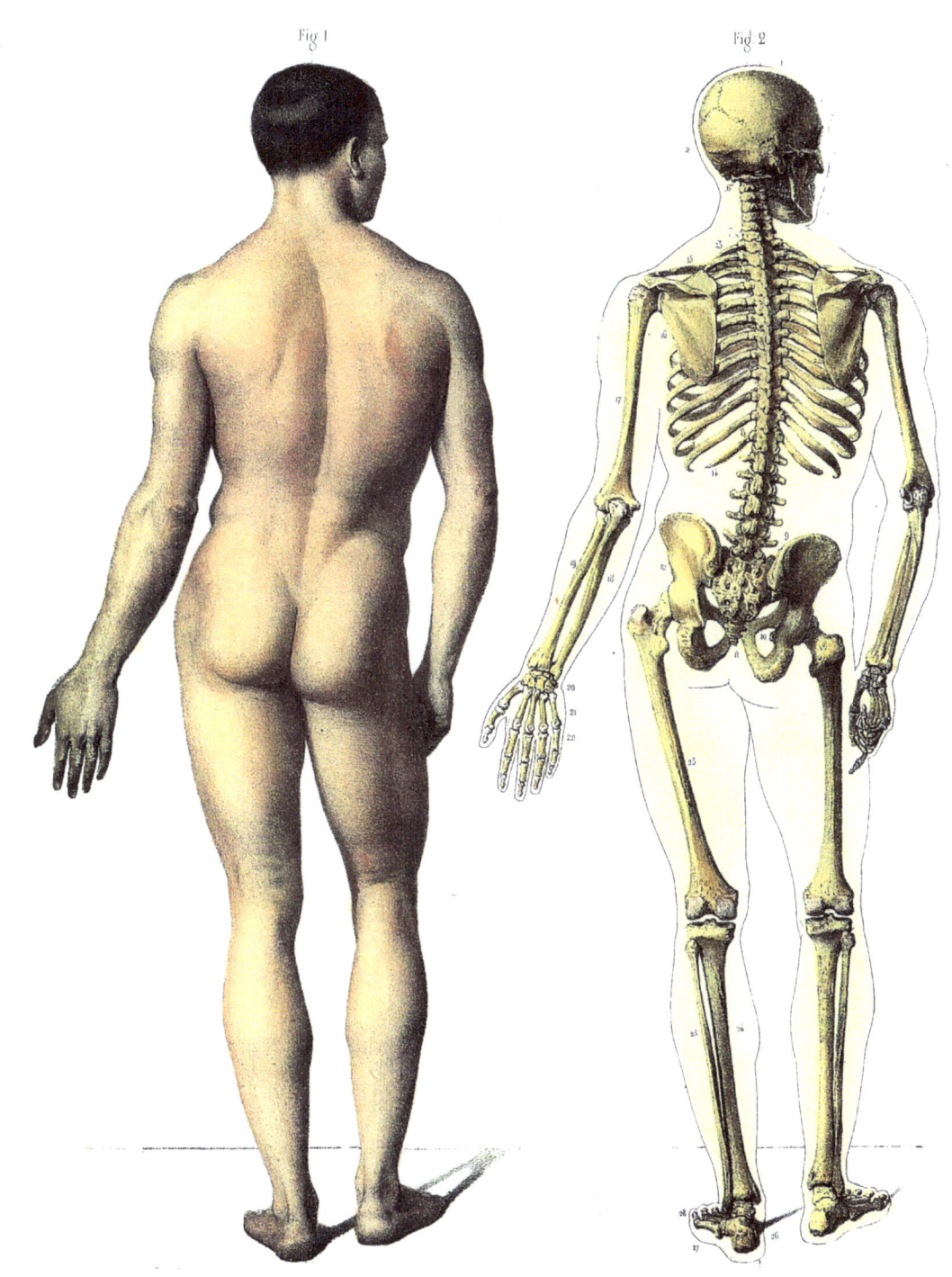

Fau 2.me edition   Paris   Imp Lemercier, Paris

MÉQUIGNON MARVIS _ GERMER BAILLI RE

PLATE III.

FIGURE 1.

1. Frontal bone.
2. Parietal.
3. Temporal.
4. Occipital.
5. Cheek bone.
6. Nasal bone.
7. Superior maxillary.
8. Lower jaw bone.
9. First cervical vertebra.
10. Seventh ditto.
11. Haunch bone.
12. Sacrum.
13. Coccyx.
14. Collar bone.
15. Sternum.
16. Scapula.
17. First rib.
18. Last rib.
19. Humerus.
20. Cubit or ulna.
21. Radius.
22. Carpus.
23. Metacarpus.
24. Phalanges.
25. Femur
26. Rotula.
27. Tibia.
28. Fibula.
29. Tarsus.
30. Metatarsus.
31. Phalanges.

FIGURE 2.

Profile of the body.

NOTE.

The student will do well to study the exact position of the male head on the neck, and to contrast it with the female. The ear is placed further forward in the female than in the male, and this holds, as Julio Romano has well shown, even in the heads of children. The balance of the female head on the neck presents in woman much more graceful forms than in the finest male proportions. On the other hand, the head and neck of the true athlete differs from the usual forms and proportions of the ordinary male figure; and the dark races have their peculiarities.

25

PL..3.

Fig 2

Fig.1

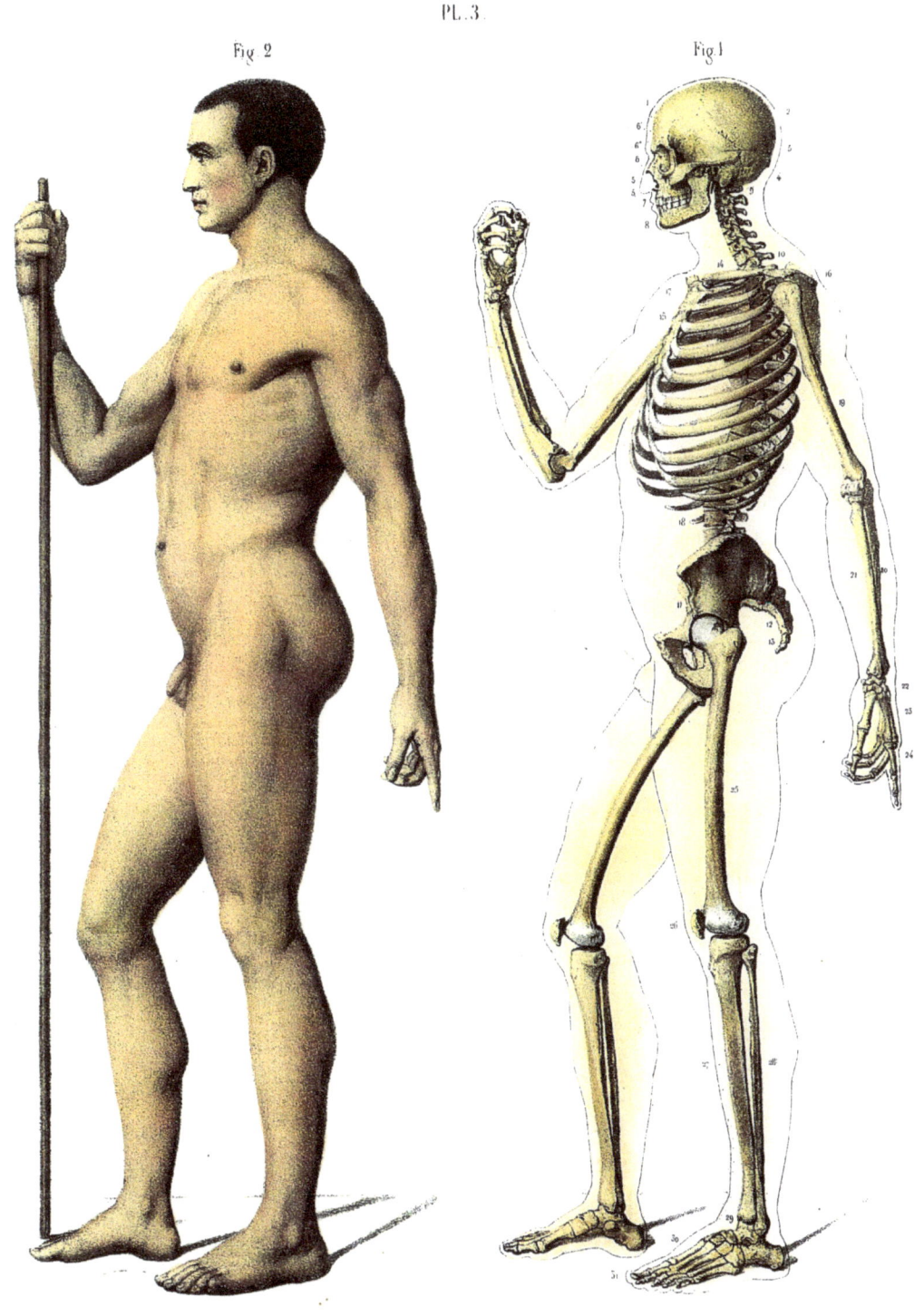

Fau 2me edition   Paris   Imp.Lemercier,Paris

MÉQUIGNON-MARVIS — GERMER BAILLIERE.

PLATES IV., V., & VI.

These drawings represent the female form, as it is frequently found in the present day, amongst the Saxon and Celtic Races of mankind. The forms here drawn are fine, but not equal to the antique, and to the rare forms which occasionally appear in the present day, resembling the antique. The antique Greek statue represents a real, and not an ideal form, as has been usually taught in schools. This I have explained in detail in the chapter containing " The Analysis of the Beautiful in Art." I need not, therefore, dwell on the details in this place. In nearly every part of these very beautiful figures, the critical eye may detect a slight deviation from the unapproachable forms of the antique ; all these deviations, as I have shown in the chapter alluded to, are so many imperfections.

In examining and drawing the infantile figures represented in these plates, the artist, and more especially the sculptor, will observe the reasons why the nude statue of the infant can never please the eye of persons of refined taste. It is wholly deficient in those grand proportions of form, in the absence of which there can exist no beauty. The sculptor will do well to consider this. The hands and feet of infants, and not unfrequently the limbs, are generally beautiful ; but not the torso. The real nature of " the beauty of youth," and why *youth*, strictly so called, is beautiful, was, as we have already seen, not understood by Winckelman, nor by any subsequent writer on the art, known to me.

Pl.4

Fig. 1.

Fig. 2

Fig. 3.

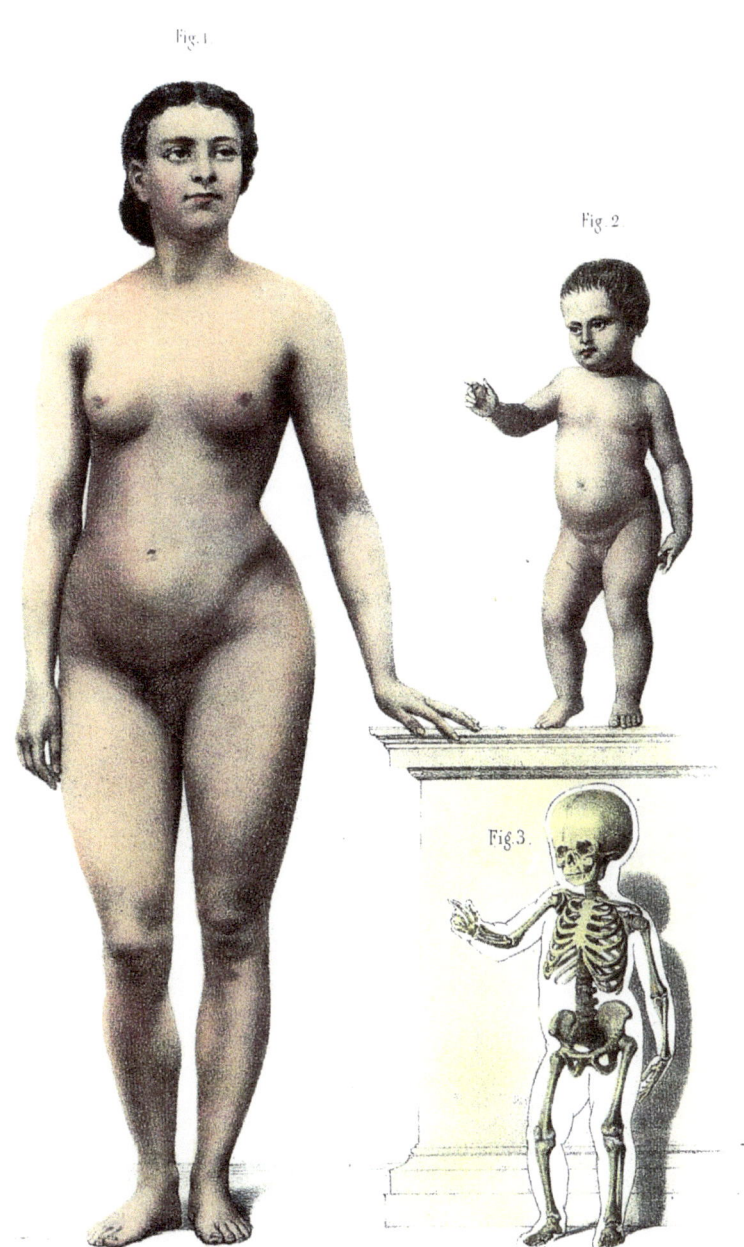

Fau . 2me édition   Paris   Imp. Lemercier et Cie Paris

MAQUIGNON-MARVIS _ GERMER BAILLIÈRE

28

Pl.5

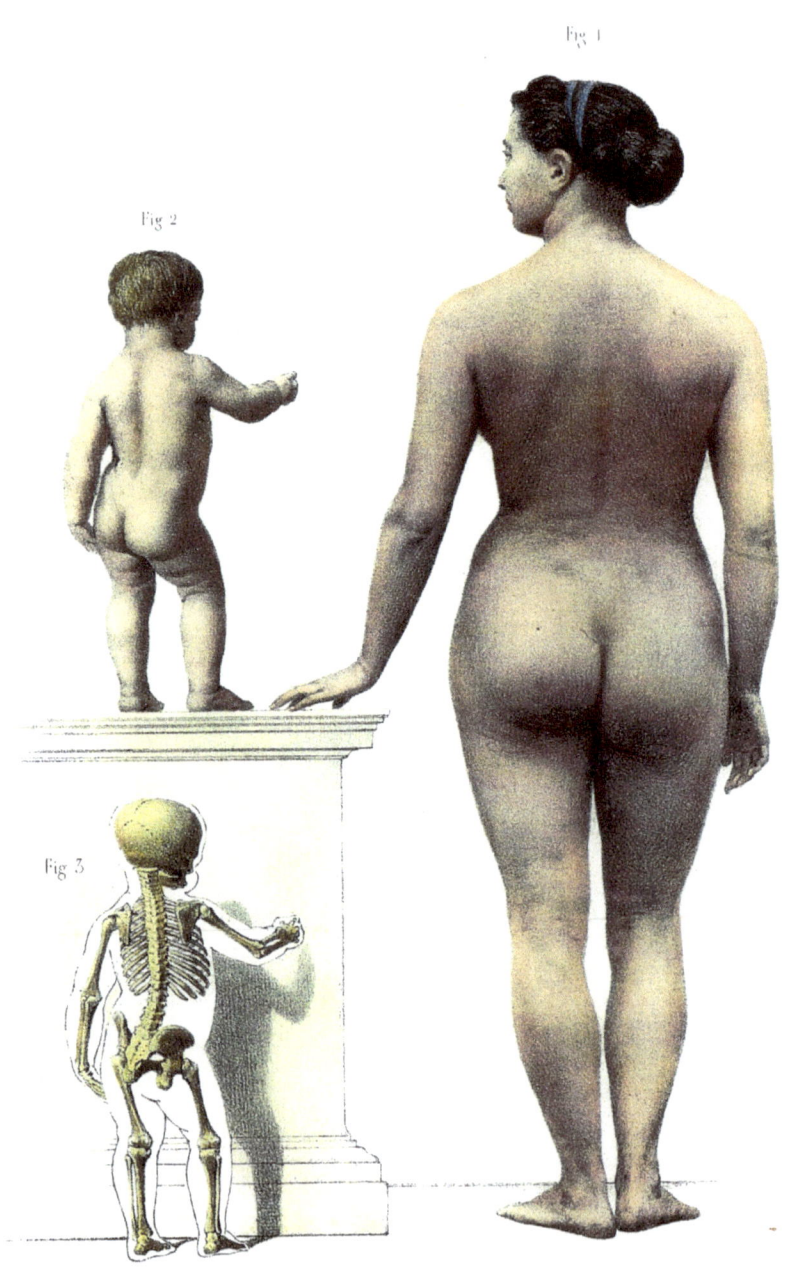

Fig 1

Fig 2

Fig 3

Fau 2.me édition   Paris   Imp Lemercier & Cie Paris
MÉQUIGNON MARVIS _ GERMER BAILLIÈRE

Pl. 6

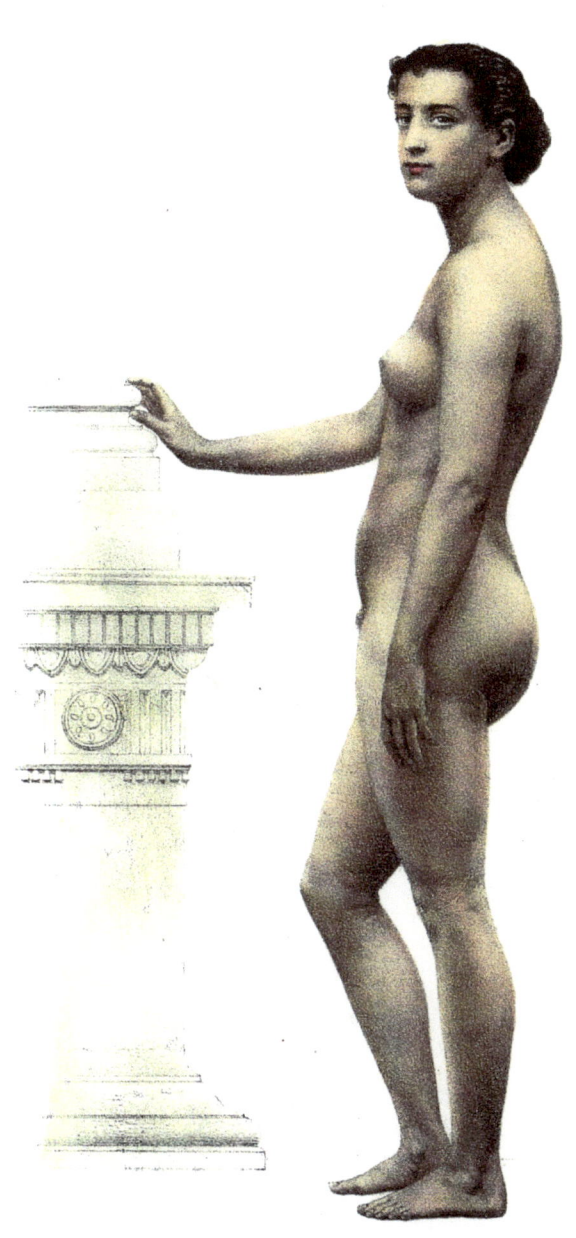

Fau 2me édition   Paris   Imp Lemercier & Cie Paris

MÉQUIGNON MARVIS _ GERMER BAILLIÈRE

PLATE VII.

FIGURE 1.

Head of the European. Facial angle, from 80° to 90°.

FIGURE 1 *bis*.

Head of the European, viewed in profile.

FIGURE 2.

Chinese Head. Facial angle, from 70° to 80°.

FIGURE 2 *bis*.

Chinese Head, viewed in profile.

FIGURE 3.

Head of the Negro of Guinea. Facial angle, from 60° to 75°.

FIGURE 3 *bis*.

Head of the Negro of Guinea, viewed in profile.

FIGURE 4.

Head of the Caraïb. Facial angle, from 60° to 70°.

FIGURE 4 *bis*.

Caraïb Head, viewed in profile.

NOTES.

The first plate contains eight lithographic engravings of the skeleton of the head and face, in four of the leading varieties, or races of men. In all these races, the female head, not represented here, differs from the male head; but most perhaps in the European. Although the skeleton of the head, and more especially that of the face, can afford to the artist but imperfect ideas of the actual form of the human face, when clothed with all its soft structures and animated with life and intelligence, it may yet be a useful exercise for the artist to draw these forms pretty frequently, in order to obtain correct notions of the osseous structures forming the basis, as it were, of the wonderful superstructure raised upon them. It will enable him also to judge more accurately of the relative proportions of the face to the cranium; of the very peculiar *setting on* of the face in the dark races of men, &c. The great size of the upper jaw bones and malar or cheek bones in the dark races, even in the Mongolian and Hindoo, will not escape his observation; this peculiarity being not at all confined to the Negro and affiliated races, as has been very generally supposed. The Caraïb Head may be taken as the type, somewhat exaggerated, of the Aboriginal Race of America. On all convenient occasions, the artistic student ought to compare these drawings with the heads themselves. Most Museums contain the actual specimens. In a word let the student recollect that in drawing these heads, he is sketching *dead forms*, not seen in *living nature*, and as I have already explained, not intended to be seen; and that these forms, if they deserve the name, have but meagre relations to the grander exterior forms with which Nature clothes and conceals the internal anatomy from human sight

Pl. 7

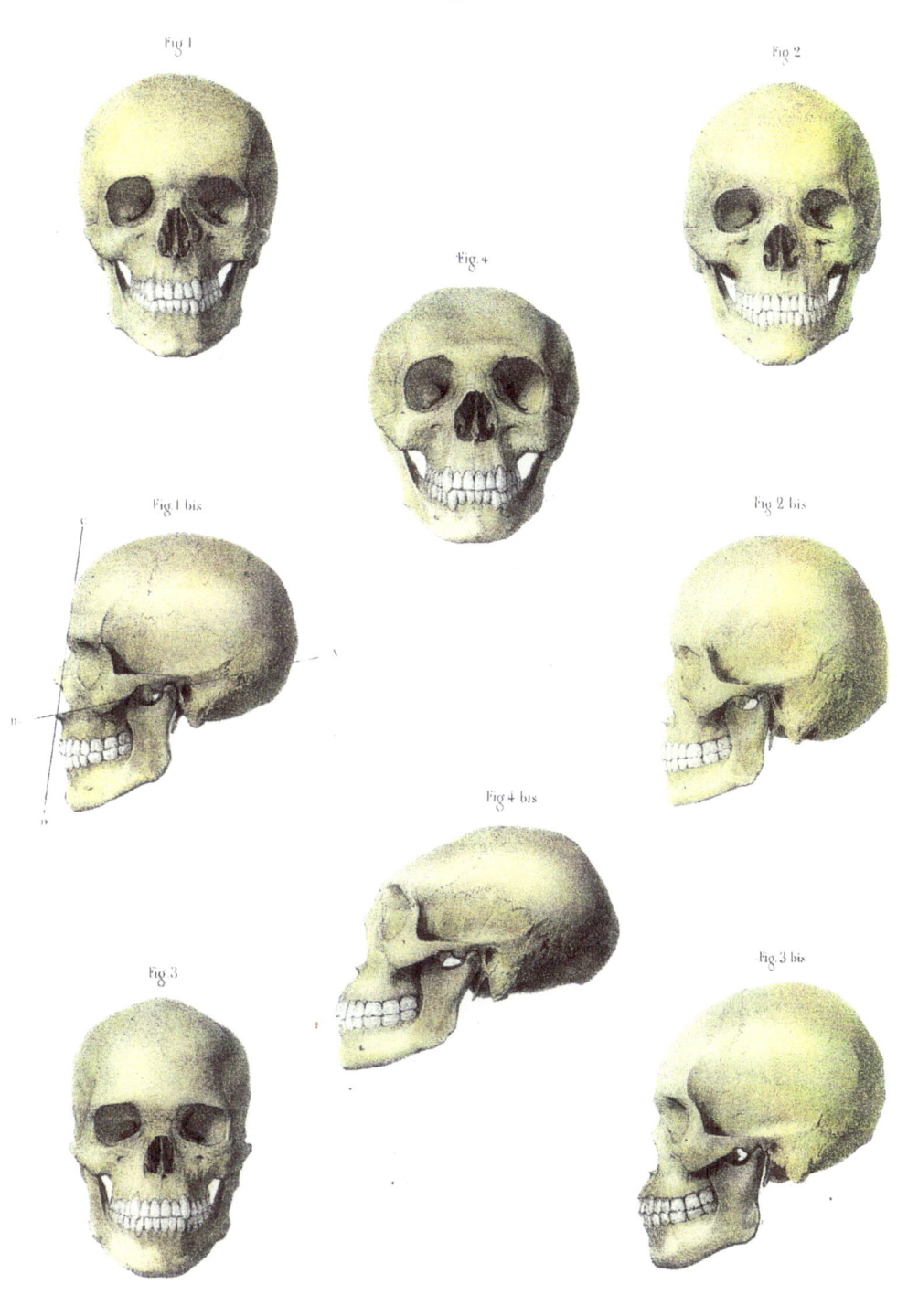

Fau 2.me édition   Paris   Imp. Lemercier Paris

M.QUIGNON MARVIS   GERMER BAILLIERE

PLATE VIII.

FIGURE 1.

A. Inferior portion of the occipital.
B. Atlas, or first vertebra of the neck.
C. Axis, or second cervical vertebra.
D. Third cervical vertebra.
E. Fourth ditto.
a. Articular surfaces of the occipital.
b. Superior *facettes* of the first vertebra.
c. Inferior *facettes*, or articular surfaces.
d. d. d. d. Transverse processes.
e. Odontoid process.
f. Superior *facettes* of the second vertebra.
g. g. Articular processes of the vertebra.
h. h. h. Bodies of the vertebra.
i. i. Articular surfaces of the bodies.

FIGURE 1 *bis.*

1. 1. Anterior cervical ligament.
2. Anterior ligament, connecting the atlas to the occipital bone.
3. Fibrous capsule, connecting the atlas and axis.
4. Capsules of the articular processes of the second, third, fourth, and fifth vertebra.
5. Divided tendons of the long muscles of the neck.

FIGURE 2.

a. a. a. a. Bodies of the seventh, eighth, ninth, and tenth vertebra.
b. b. b. b. Costo-vertebral *facettes.*
c. c. c. c. Superior and inferior *facettes.*
d. d. d. d. Spinous processes.
e. e. e. e. Transverse processes.
f. f. f. f. Articular tubercles of the ribs.

FIGURE 2 *bis.*

1. 1. Common anterior vertebral ligament.
2. 2. 2. Inter-articular discs, or inter-vertebral fibro-cartilages.
3. Costo-vertebral ligaments.
4. Inferior costo-transverse ligaments.
5. Inter-spinous dorsal ligaments.
6. 6. Supra-spinous dorsal ligament.

FIGURE 3.

A. Collar bone.
B. Shoulder blade.
C. Humerus, or arm bone.
a. Sterno-clavicular articular *facette,* or articular surface of the collar bone where it meets the breast bone.

b. Acromio-clavicular articular *facette, i.e.,* the articular surface by which the collar bone meets the acromion process of the scapula.
c. Acromion process.
d. Its *facette,* or articular surface.
e. Coracoid process.
f. Glenoid cavity.
g. Articular surface of the head of the humerus.
h. Bicipital groove.

FIGURE 3 *bis.*

1. Anterior coraco-clavicular aponeurotic fasciculus, a bundle of aponeurotic fibres, extending from the coracoid process to the collar bone.
2. Anterior coraco-clavicular ligament.
3. Coraco-acromial ligament.
4. Scapulo-clavicular fibrous capsule.
5. Scapulo-coracoid ligament.
6. Coraco-humeral ligament.
7. Scapulo-humeral fibrous capsule.
8. Tendon of the sub-scapular muscle.
9. Tendon of the biceps muscle.
10. Tendon of the long portion of the triceps muscle.

FIGURE 4.

A. Collar bone.
B. Scapula.
C. Humerus.
a. Acromion process.
b. Coracoid process.
c. Spine of the scapula.
d. Glenoid cavity.
e. Articular surface of the humerus.

FIGURE 4 *bis.*

1. Posterior coraco-clavicular aponeurotic fasciculus.
2. Inferior coraco-clavicular ligaments.
3. Scapulo-coracoid capsule.
4. Scapulo-coracoid ligament.
5. Capsule of the joint.
6. Attachments of the supra-spinatus, infra-spinatus, and teres minor muscles.
7. Tendon of the long portion of the triceps.

FIGURE 5.

A. Humerus.
B. Ulna, or cubit.
C. Radius.
D. Bones of the hand.
a. Sigmoid fossette.

34

b. Inner condyle of the humerus.
c. Outer condyle of ditto.
d. The trochlea or pulley.
e. Smaller head of the humerus.
f. Olecranon process.
g. Articular cavity of the cubit.
h. Sigmoid process.
i. Superior articular facette.
j. Rough surface, for the attachment of the brachialis flexor muscle.
k. Inferior articular facette.
l. Styloid process of the ulna.
m. Head of the radius and its two articular surfaces.
n. Bicipital tuberosity.
o. Inferior articular facette.
p. Styloid process of the radius.
b. Scaphoid bone.
r. Semi-lunar bone.
s. Pyramidal bone.
t. Pisiform bone.
u. Trapezium bone.
v. Trapezoid bone.
x. Os magnum.
y. Unciform bone.
z. The five bones of the metacarpus.
z'. The first five phalanges.
z''. Last phalanx of the thumb.

Note.—I know not why M. Fau has omitted in this Figure, and also in Figure 6, the last phalanges of the fingers ; that is, the bones supporting the nails.

FIGURE 5 *bis.*

1. Anterior ligament of the elbow joint.
2. Internal lateral ligament.
3. External lateral ligament.
4. Tendon of the biceps.
5. Inter-osseous ligament.
6. Anterior, inferior cubito-radial ligament.
7. Great anterior radio-carpal ligament.
8. Internal lateral ligament.
9. External lateral ligament.
10. Ligaments of the carpus.
11. Fibrous capsule, uniting the trapezium to the first metacarpal bone.
12. Palmar inter-osseous ligaments.
13. Tendon of the posterior cubital muscle.
14. Tendon of the long abductor muscle of the thumb.
15. Transverse metacarpal ligaments.
16. Articular ligament and capsule of the thumb.
17. Index finger and fibrous sheath of the tendons.

18. Medius ; the tendons of the superficial and deep flexors have been exposed by dissection.
19. Ring finger ; the tendons have been removed by dissection.
20. Little finger ; with the capsule, called metacarpo-phalangean, laid open.

FIGURE 6.

A. The humerus.
B. The cubit or ulna.
C. Radius.
D. Bones of the hand.
a. Olecranian facette.
b. Inner condyle of the humerus.
c. Outer condyle of the humerus.
d. Trochlea or pulley.
e. Olecranon.
f. Styloid process of the cubit.
g. Head of the radius, and its articular surfaces.
h. Styloid process of the radius.
i. i. Grooves for the extensor tendons, separated by a small process of bone.
j. Scaphoid bone.
k. Semi lunar bone.
l. Pyramidal bone.
m. Pisiform bone.
n. Trapezium bone.
o. Trapezoid bone.
p. Os magnum bone.
q. Unciform bone.
r. Bones of the metacarpus.
s. First phalanges.
t. Last phalanx of the thumb.

FIGURE 6 *bis.*

1. Posterior humero-cubital ligament.
2. Internal lateral ligament of the elbow.
3. External lateral ligament.
4. Annular ligament in which the radius moves.
5. Inter-osseus ligament.
6. Posterior and inferior cubito-radial ligament.
7. Great posterior radio-carpal ligament.
8. Internal lateral ligament of the wrist.
9. External ligament.
10. Ligament of the carpus.
11. Fibrous capsule of the first metacarpal bone.
12. Dorsal inter-osseus ligaments.
13. Tendon of the posterior cubital muscle,
14. Tendon of the long abductor of the thumb.
15. Tendons of the radial muscles.
16. Transverse metacarpal ligament.
17. 17. Fingers with their ligaments and capsules.

Pl. 8

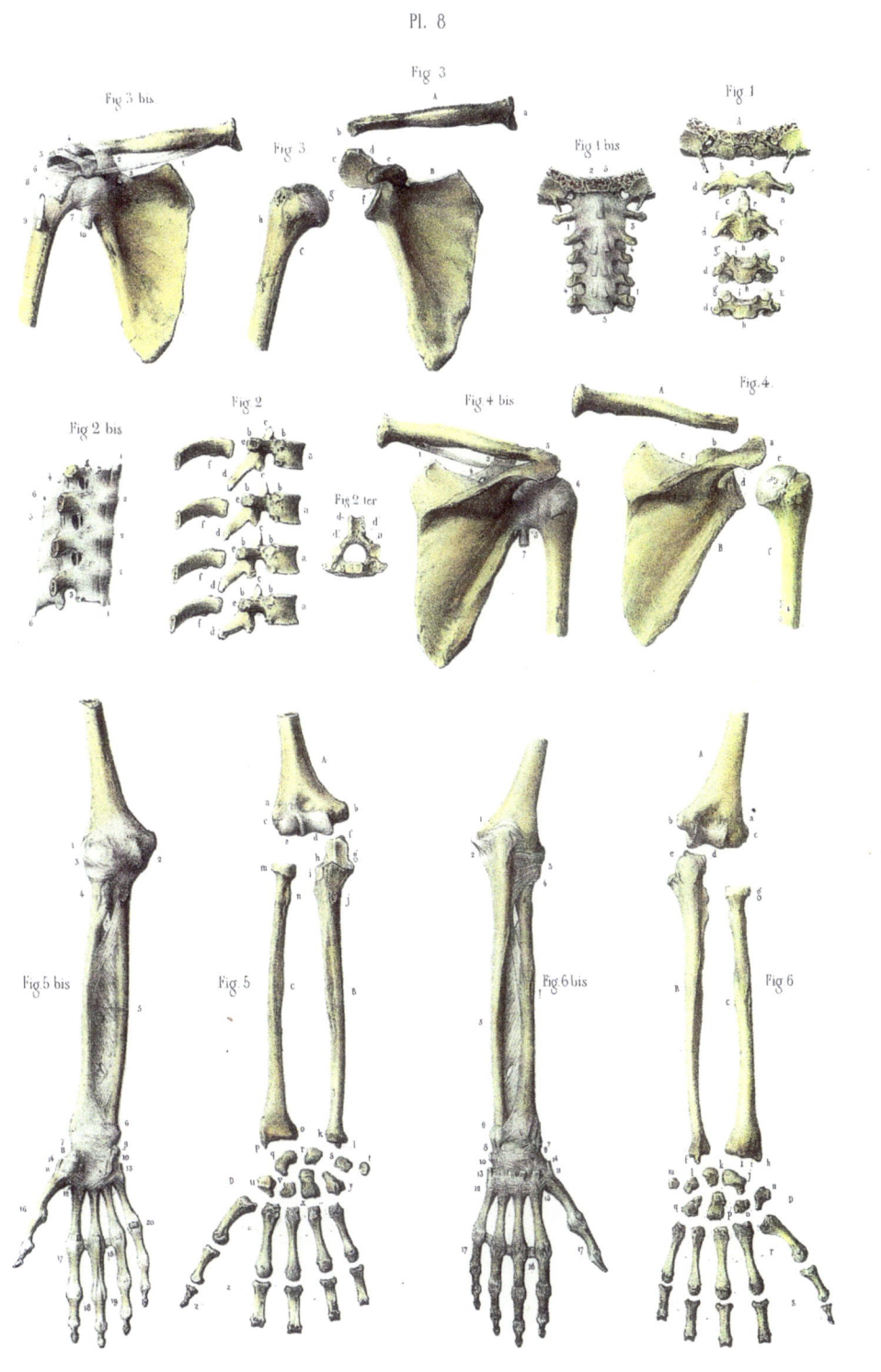

Fait 2.me édition.

Paris

Imp.Lemercier,Paris

MÉQUIGNON MARVIS   GERMER BAILLIÈRE.

PLATE IX.

FIGURE 1.

A. Inferior portion of the cranium.
B. Branch of the jaw.
a. Zygomatic arch.
b. Glenoid cavity.
c. Mastoid process.
d. Condyle of the jaw.
e. Coronoid process.
f. Angle of the jaw.
g. Orifice of the auditory canal.
h. Styloid process.

FIGURE 1 *bis.*

1. External lateral ligament.
2. Stylo-maxillary ligament.

FIGURE 2.

a. a. a. Bodies of the second, third, and fourth lumbar vertebra.
b. b. b. Articular surfaces.
c. c. c. Transverse processes.
d. d. d. Superior inferior articular processes.
e. e. e. Spinous processes.

FIGURE 2 *bis.*

First, second, third and fourth lumbar vertebra.
1. Crus or pillar of the midriff, or diaphragm.
2. Anterior common vertebral ligament.
3. Radiated ligament.
4. 4. Inter-vertebral discs, or fibro-cartilages.
5. Articulo-transverse ligaments.
6. Tendon of the transverse spinous muscle, lumbar portion.
7. Inter-spinous ligaments, and tendons of the long muscles of the back.
8. 8. Supra-spinous ligaments.
9. Articular capsule laid open.

FIGURE 3.

A. Haunch bones.
B. Sacrum.
C. Coccyx.
D. Lumbar vertebra.
E. Femur.
a. Ilion.
b. Ischion.
c. Pubis.
d. Iliac crest, terminated by the superior spine.
e. Inferior spine.
f. Articular surface.
g. Cotyloid artery.
h. Articular surface of the head of the femur.
i. Round ligament.
j. Great trochanter.
k. Small trochanter.

FIGURE 3 *bis.*

1. Disc.
2. Ilio-lumbar ligament.
3. Anterior sacro-iliac ligament.
4. Sacro-sciatic ligament.
5. Anterior sacro-coccygeal ligament.
6. Cross-shaped ligaments of the pubis, covering the symphysis.
7. Sub-pubic ligament.
8. Articular fibro-capsule, with its strengthening fasciculus.
9. Tendon of the rectus muscle.
10. Gluteus medius.
11. Gluteus minimus.
12. Triceps.
Note.—The tendinous attachments of these muscles alone are seen here.

FIGURE 4.

A. Coxal bone.
B. Sacrum.
C. The coccyx.
D. Femur.
a. Iliac crest.
b. Sciatic spine.
c. Sciatic tuberosity.
d. Articular surface.
e. Spinous process.
f. Head and articular surface of the femur.
g. Neck of the bone.
h. Great trochanter.
i. Small trochanter.
j. Articular surface of the sacrum.

FIGURE 4 *bis.*

1. Posterior sacro-iliac ligament.
2. Great sacro-sciatic ligament.
3. Posterior sacro-coccygeal ligament.
4. Sub-pubic (obturator) ligament.
5. Fibrous capsule.
6. Tendinous attachment of the gluteus minimus.
7. Tendon of the gluteus medius.
8. Tendons of the biceps and semi-tendinosus muscles.
9. Third adductor.

FIGURE 5.

A Femur.
B. Tibia.
C. Fibula.
D. Rotula.
a. Inner tuberosity.
b. Outer tuberosity.
c. Articular notch.
d. Spine of the tibia.

38

e. e. Articular surfaces.
f. Inner tuberosity.
g. Outer tuberosity.
h. Tuberosity of the tibia.
i. Articular surface of the fibula.

FIGURE 5 *bis.*

1. Triceps.
2. Tendon, or ligament of the rotula.
3. Internal lateral ligament of the rotula.
4. External ligament.
5. External lateral ligament of the articulation.
6. Internal lateral ligament.
7. Tendon of the aponeurosis of the fascia lata.
8. Inter-osseous ligament.
9. Tendon of the third adductor.
10. Tendon of the biceps.
11. Tendons of the internal muscles of the thigh.

FIGURE 6.

A. Femur.
B. Tibia.
C. Fibula.
a. Inner tuberosity.
b. Outer tuberosity.
c. Inner condyle.
d. Outer condyle.
e. Spine of the tibia.
f. Articular surfaces.
g. Articular facette.
h. Articular surface of the rotula.

FIGURE 6 *bis.*

1. Posterior superficial ligament.
2. Internal lateral ligament.
3. External lateral ligament.
4. Posterior peroneo-tibial ligament.
5. Inter-osseous ligament.
6. Attachment of the third adductor.
7. 7. Attachment of the gastro-cnemius internus and plantaris gracilis.
8. Attachment of the popliteus.
9. Attachment of the biceps.
10. Attachment of the soleus.
11. Attachment of the peroneus longus.

FIGURE 6 *ter.*

1. 1. Semi-lunar fibro-cartilages.
2. 2. Articular surfaces of the tibia.
3. Anterior crucial ligament.
4. Posterior ditto.
5. Ligament of the rotula.

FIGURE 7.

A. Tibia.
B. Fibula.
C. Astragalus.
D. Calcaneum.
E. Scaphoid.
F. Cuboid.
G. Great cuneiform.

H. Small cuneiform.
I. Middle cuneiform.
J. Bones of the metatarsus.
a. Malleolus internus.
a'. External malleolus.
b. Articular surfaces of the tibia, fibula, and astragalus.
c. Attachment of the tendon achilles.
d. d. Articulation of the calcaneum with the astragalus.
e. Articulation with the cuboid.

FIGURE 7 *bis.*

1. Inter-osseus ligament.
2. Inferior peroneo-tibial ligaments.
3. Anterior tibio-tarsal ligament.
4. Internal lateral ligament.
5. External lateral ligament.
6. Peroneo-astragalian ligament.
7. Ligaments of the tarsus.
8. Transverse metatarsal ligament.
9. Attachment of the tibialis anticus muscle.
10. Attachment of the peroneus brevis muscle.
11. Attachment of the adductor muscle of the great toe.
12. Tendons of the long extensor muscles of the toes; the tendinous sheaths; the articulation of the fourth toe has been laid open.

FIGURE 8.

A. Calcaneum.
B. Malleolus externus.
1. Inferior calcaneo-cuboid ligament.
2. Groove for the long proper flexor of the great toe.
3. Groove for the long common flexor muscle.
4. Cuneo-metatarsal ligament.
5. Transverse metatarsal ligament.
6. Tibialis posticus.
7. Tibialis anticus.
8. Peroneus longus.
9. Peroneus brevis.
10. Adductor of the little toe.
11. Short flexor of the little toe.
12. Adductor and short flexor of the great toe.
13. Oblique adductor of the great toe.
14. Toes, sheaths, tendons of the long flexor; the joint of the fourth toe has been laid open.

FIGURE 9.

A. Malleolus internus.
B. External malleolus.
C. Calcaneum and tendo-achilles.
1. Inter-osseous ligament.
2. Posterior ligament of the inferior peroneo-tibial articulation.
3. Posterior peroneo-astragalian ligament.
4. External lateral ligament.
5. Internal lateral ligament.
6. Sheath of the common flexor tendons of the toes.
7. Sheath of the tibialis posticus.
8. Sheath of the tendons of the peronei muscles.

Pl. 9

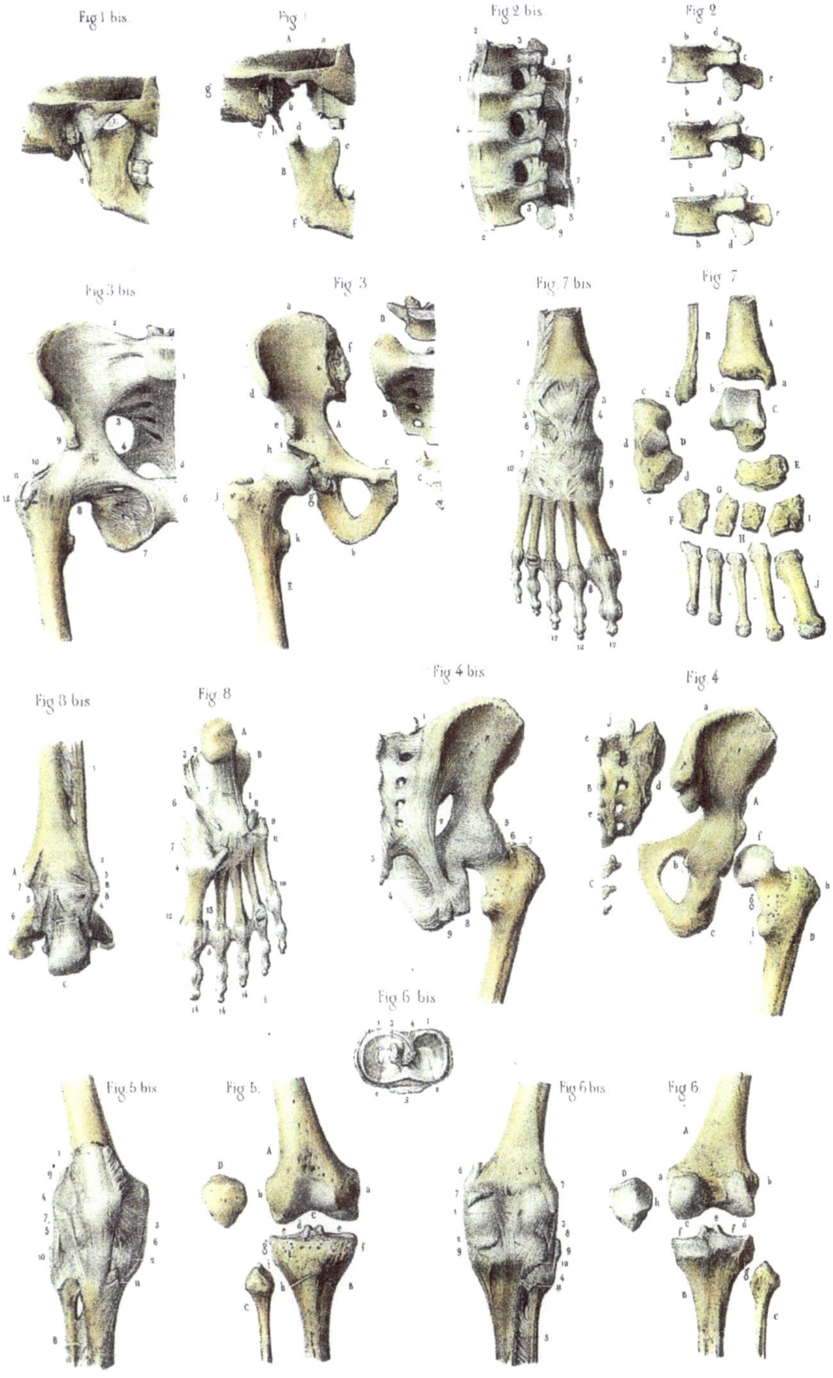

Fig 1 bis   Fig 1   Fig 2 bis   Fig 2

Fig 3 bis   Fig 3   Fig 7 bis   Fig 7

Fig 3 bis   Fig 8   Fig 4 bis   Fig 4

Fig 6 bis

Fig 5 bis   Fig 5.   Fig 6 bis   Fig 6.

Fou   2.me édition   Paris   Imp Lemer ier,Paris
MÉQUIGNON MARVIS   GERMER BAILLIÈRE.

PLATE X.

The numerous muscles of the head, with forms so varied and arrangements altogether peculiar, present great difficulties to the student. The researches of M. Cruveilhier have, no doubt, considerably simplified their study; nevertheless, we should require to enter into too many details were we to attempt succinctly indicating to the artist the attachments of these muscles, so united together as to form, as it were, but one, whose fasciculi so mingle and cross each other as to constitute a muscular net-work spread over the face, adhering on one side to the skin, on the other to bones and aponeuroses. I shall limit myself, therefore, to the pointing out merely the points of attachment of the occipito-frontal, the temporal and masseter muscles, referring the student for all other details to strictly anatomical works, and especially to the excellent Treatise on Descriptive Anatomy, by M. Cruveilhier. Besides, the engravings will give a sufficiently accurate idea of the situation of all these muscles, whose diverse actions I have already described in Chapter ix., § 3.

FIGURE 1.

A. Frontal bone.
B. Parietal bone.
C. Malar bone.
D. Upper jaw bone.
E. Lower jaw bone.
F. Seventh vertebra of the neck.
G. First rib.
H. Collar bone.

FIGURE 2.

A. Frontal bone.
B. Malar bone.
E. Lower jaw bone.
H. Collar bone.
I. Frontal portion of the occipito-frontalis muscle.

Attachments.—To the epicranial aponeurosis, interlacing with the orbicular muscle of the eyelids; also, to the dorsal aponeurosis of the nose, and is continuous with the pyramidalis muscle.

2. Orbicular muscle of the eyelids.
3. Triangular of the nose; the pyramidal is above it.
4. Common elevator of the upper lip and nose.
5. Proper elevator of the upper lip.
6. Smaller zygomatic.
7. Larger zygomatic.
8. Orbicular of the lips.
9. Triangular muscle of the chin.
10. Square muscle of the chin.
11. Elevator of the chin.
12. Masseter muscle.

Attachments.—1°. To the inferior margin of the zygomatic arch.

2. To the external surface of the ramus or branch, and of the angle of the lower jaw bone, and to the same surface of the coronoid process.

13. Broadest muscle of the neck. (*See* Pl. ix. and x., Fig. 4.) The lattissimus colli of anatomists.*

14. Sterno-cleido mastoideus.

Attachments.—1°. To the inner portion of the collar bone, and to the upper and anterior part of the breast bone.

2°. To the mastoid process, and to the upper curved line of the occipital bone.

15. Sterno-thyroideus muscle. (*See* Pl. ix. Fig. 5.)

16. Omo-thyroideus. (*See* Pl. ix., Fig. 5.)

17. Trapezius. (*See* Pl. xi.)

FIGURE 3.

A. Frontal bone.
B. Parietal bone.
C. Occipital bone.
D. Bones of the nose.
E. Malar bone.
F. Upper jaw bone.
G. Lower jaw bone.
H. Seventh vertebra of the neck.
I. First rib.
J. Collar bone.
K. Breast bone.
L. Spine of the scapula and acromion process.

FIGURE 4.

This drawing represents the superficial layer of muscles.

1. Anterior auricular
2. Superior auricular.
4. Parotid gland.
5. Muscular risorius of Santorini.

---

* The French call this muscle *peauoier;* it is a remarkable muscle, strongly developed in some persons, but not in the ratio of their general muscular development. It forms a portion of a dermoid system of muscles, which in the horse and some other animals, covers a large portion of the trunk.

FIGURE 5.

A. Frontal bone.

B. Parietal bone.

C. Occipital bone.

E. Malar or cheek bone.

G. Lower jaw bone.

I. Collar bone.

L. Spine of the scapula.

M. Lingual or tongue bones.

1. Frontal portion of the occipito frontal muscle.

1¹. Occipital portion of the same muscle.

Attachments.—1°. To the two external thirds of the superior occipital curved line, and to the mastoid region of the temporal bone.

2°. To the epicranial aponeurosis.

2. Temporal muscle.

Attachments.—1°. To all the temporal fossa, and to the superficial temporal aponeurosis.

2°. To the coronoid process of the lower jaw bone.

3. Orbicular muscle of the eyelids.

4. Triangular of the nose.

5. Common elevator of the ala, or wing of the nose, and upper lip, and proper elevator of the upper lip.

6. Small zygomatic.

7. Large zygomatic.

8. Orbicular muscle of the lips.

9. Triangular muscle of the chin.

10. Square muscle of the chin.

11. Buccinator.

12. Masseter.

13. Sterno-cleido mastoid.

14. Splenius muscle.

Attachments.—1°. To the spinous processes of four or five of the uppermost dorsal vertebræ, of the sixth and seventh vertebræ of the neck, and to the lower portion of the cervical ligament.

2°. To the transverse processes of two or three of the uppermost vertebræ of the neck, to the back part of the mastoid process, and to the superior curved line of the occipital bone.

15. Levator muscle of the angle of the scapula.

Attachments.—1°. To the transverse processes of the four or five uppermost cervical vertebræ.

2°. To the superior angle of the scapula, and to the inner margin of the same bone, above the scapular spine.

16. Posterior scalenus muscle.

Attachments.—1°. To the first rib.

2°. To the transverse processes of the six lowermost cervical vertebræ.

17. Anterior scalenus muscle.

Attachments.—To the first rib.

2°. To the transverse processes of the third, fourth, fifth, and sixth vertebræ of the neck.

18. Trapezius muscle. (*See* Pl. xi.)

19. Digastric muscle.

Attachments.—1°. To the mastoid process.

2°. To the base of the lower jaw bone, near the symphysis of the chin, and to the lingual bones.

20. Mylo-hyoideus muscle.

Attachments.—1°. To the mylo-hyoidien line.

2°. To the lingual or hyoid bones.

21. Sterno-hyoideus.

Attachments.—1°. To the inner end of the collar bone, and to the outer part of the sternum.

2°. To the lower margin of the body of the lingual bones.

21. Omo-hyoideus muscle.

Attachments.—1°. To the upper margin of the scapula, behind the coracoid notch.

2°. To the inferior margin of the body of the lingual bones.

23. Thyro-hyoideus muscle.

Attachments.—1°. To the thyroid cartilage of the larynx.

2°. To the body and large horn of the lingual bone.

Pl. 10

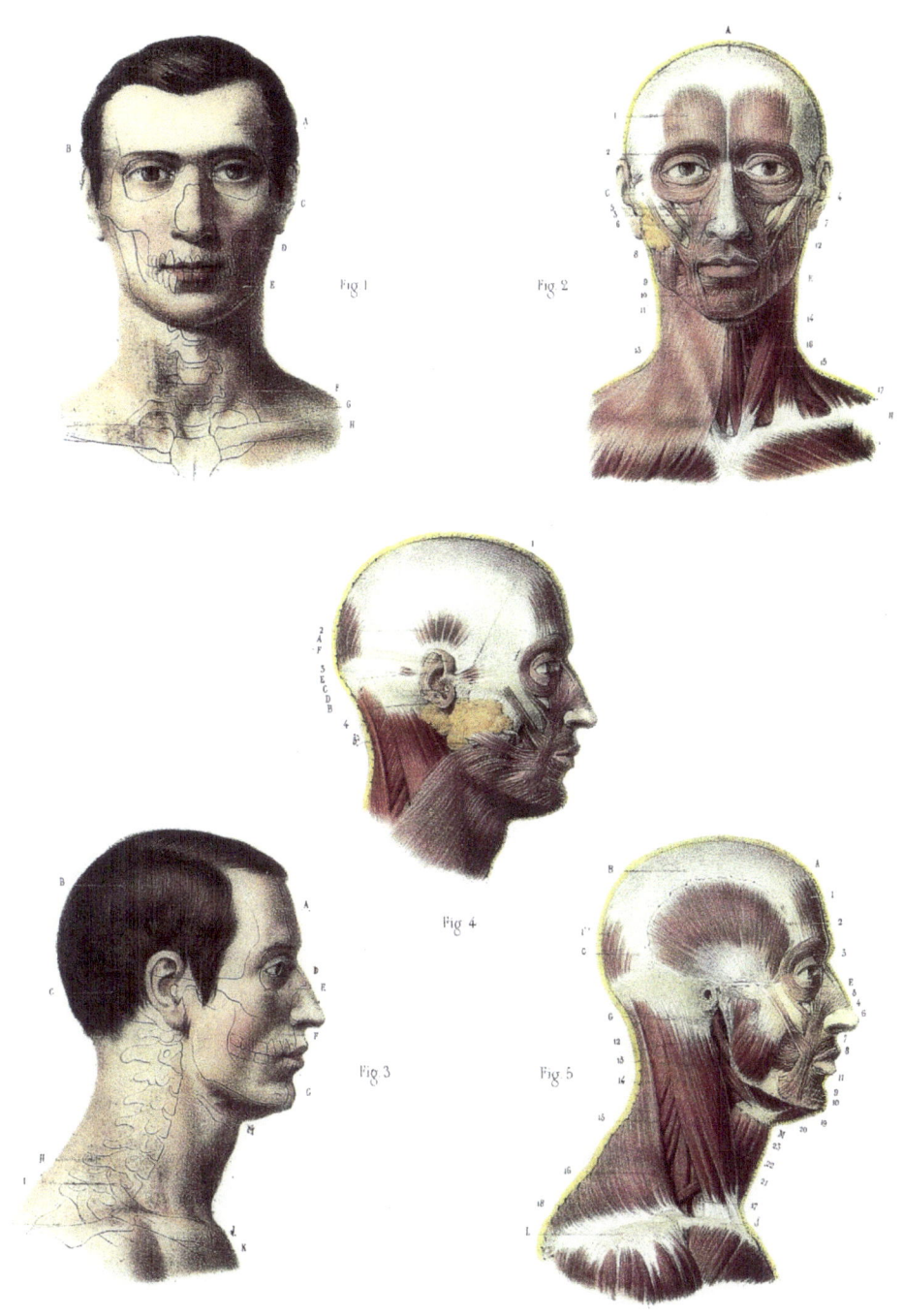

Fig 1

Fig 2

Fig 4

Fig 3

Fig 5

Fau 2.me édition   Paris   Imp.Lemercier,Paris

MÉQUIGNON MARVIS _ GERMER BAILLIÈRE.

PLATE XI.

FIGURE 1.

A. Last cervical vertebra.
B. Collar bone.
C. Scapula and its appendages.
D. Breast bone.
E. First rib.
F. Seventh rib.
G. Twelfth rib.
H. Twelfth vertebra of the back.
I. Last lumbar vertebra.
J. Sacrum and coccyx.
K. Coxal or haunch bone.
L. Humerus.
M. Femur.

FIGURE 2.

B. Collar bone.
D. Breast bone.
K. Anterior and superior iliac spine and pubis.
1. Latissimus colli and risorius muscle of Santorini.

Attachments.—1°. To the skin of the anterior and superior part of the chest.
2°. To the lower jaw bone, and to the skin of the face.

2. Sterno - cleido mastoideus muscle. (*See* Pl. ix.)
3. Sterno-hyoïdeus. (*See* Pl. ix.)
4. Digastricus. (*See* Pl. ix.)
5. Omo-hyoïdeus. (*See* Pl. ix.)
6. Trapezius. (*See* Pl. xi.)

7. Deltoides. (*See* Pl. xii.)
8. Great pectoral muscle.

Attachments.—1°. To the anterior margin of the collar bone, to the anterior surface of the sternum, to the cartilages of the second, third, fourth, fifth, and sixth ribs, to the body of the sixth rib, and to the abdominal aponeurosis.
2°. To the anterior edge of the bicipital groove of the humerus.

9. Serratus magnus muscle. (*See* Pl. xii.)
10. Great oblique muscle. (*See* Pl. xii.)
11. Latissimus dorsi. (*See* Pl. xii.)
12. Rectus or straight muscle of the abdomen.

Attachments.—1°. To the cartilages of the fifth, sixth and seventh ribs, and to the sternum.
2°. To the upper margin of the pubis, between the spine and symphisis.

13. Pyramidalis muscle.

Attachments.—1°. To the linea alba.
2°. To the pubis, anterior to the rectus. This muscle is often wanting.

14. Tensor fasciæ latæ. (*See* Pl. xxi.)
15. Rectus cruris.
16. Sartorius; the muscle in the other limb is enclosed by the aponeurosis.
17. Pectineus. An abductor muscle.
18. First abductor.
19. Testicular, or spermatic cord.

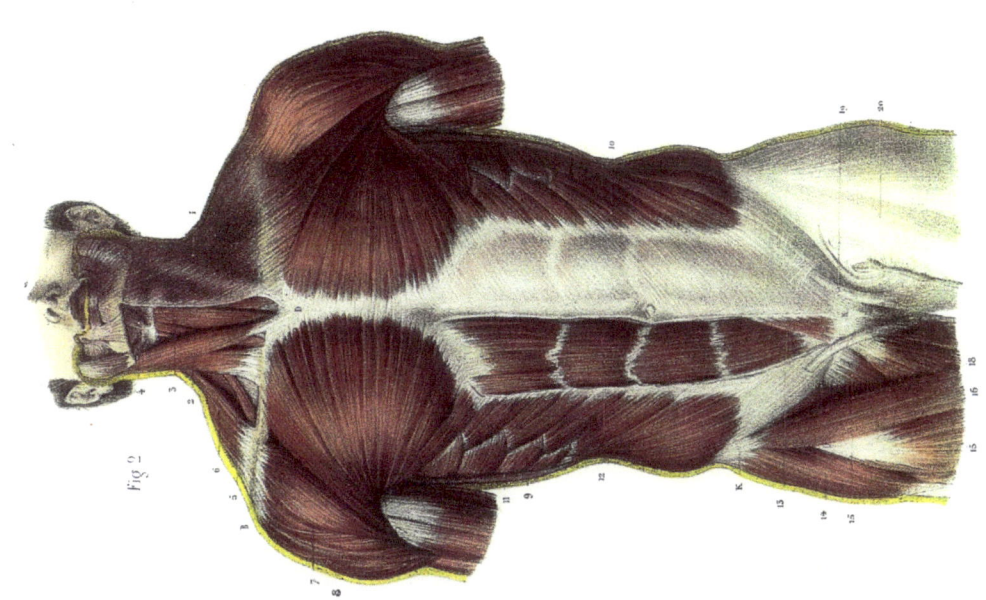

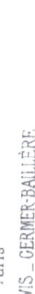

Fig 2.

Pl. II

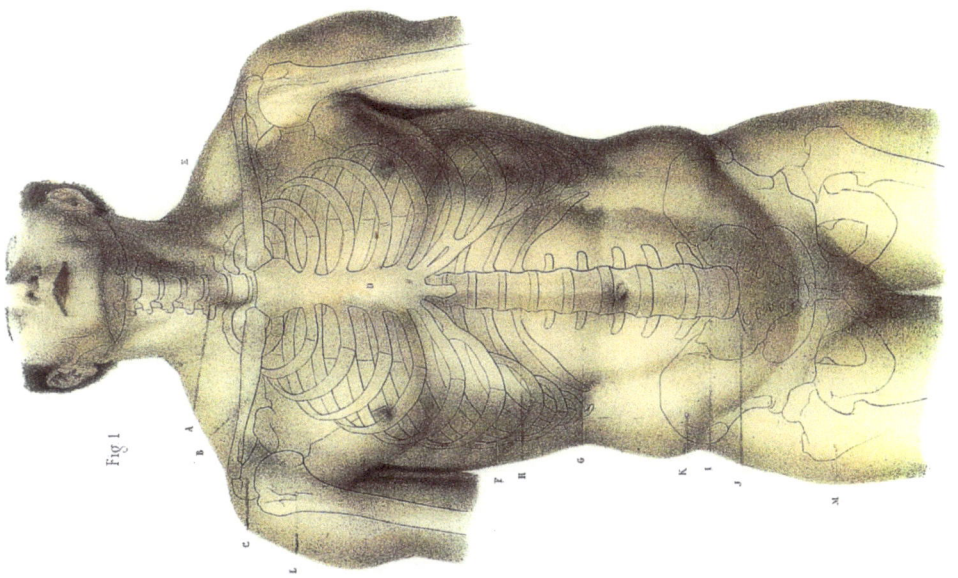

Fig 1.

Imp. Lemercier et C.ie Paris

Paris

MÉQUIGNON-MARVIS _ GERMER-BAILLIÈRE

Fau _ 2.me édiuon.

PLATE XII.

FIGURE 1.

A. Occiput.
B. First cervical vertebra.
C. Seventh cervical vertebra.
D. Twelfth dorsal.
E. Fifth lumbar.
F. Sacrum and coccyx.
G. Coxal or haunch bone.
H. First rib.
I. Twelfth rib.
J. Collar bone.
K. Scapula.
L. Humerus.
M. Femur.

FIGURE 2.

C. Seventh cervical vertebra.
K. Spine of the scapula.
M. Great trochanter.
1. Occipital muscle. (*See* Pl. ix.)
2. Sterno-cleido mastoideus. (*See* Pl. ix.)
3. Splenius muscle. (*See* Pl. ix.)
4. Trapezius muscle.

Attachments.—1°. To the inner third of the superior curved occipital line, to the external occipital protuberance, to the posterior cervical ligament, the spinous processes of the sixth and seventh cervical vertebra, to the ten uppermost of, and sometimes to the spinous processes of all the dorsal vertebra.

2°. To the margin of the scapular spine throughout its whole length to the posterior margin of the acromion process, to the outer third of the posterior margin of the collar bone.

5. Deltoid muscle. (*See* Pl. xii.)
6. Triceps.
7. Infra-spinatus muscle.

Attachments.—1°. To the two inner thirds of the infra-spinous fossa, and its aponeuroses.

2°. To the middle portion of the larger tuberosity of the humerus.

The supra-spinatus muscle, which is not seen here, is attached on one hand to the two inner thirds of the supra-spinatus fossa; and on the other to the superior portion of the larger tuberosity of the humerus.

8. Teres minor muscles.

Attachments.—1°. To the infra-spinous fossa, near the margin (external) of the scapula, and to its aponeuroses.

2°. To the inferior part of the larger tuberosity of the humerus.

9. Teres major muscle.

Attachments.—1°. To the posterior portion of the inferior angle of the scapula, and to the aponeurotic partitions.

2°. To the posterior margin of the bicipital groove of the humerus.

10. Rhomboid muscle.

Attachments.—1°. To the inferior part of the cervical ligament, to the spinous processes of the seventh cervical vertebra, and of the first five dorsal.

2°. To the inferior portion of the inner margin of the scapula.

11. Great dorsal, or latissimus dorsi muscle.

Attachments.—1°. To the spinous processes of the six or seven last dorsal vertebra, of the lumbar and sacral vertebra, and to the four last ribs. It interlocks with the great oblique muscle.

2°. To the bottom of the bicipital groove of the humerus.

12. The fleshy masses, called sacro-lumbar, composed of the muscles called sacro-lumbar, longest of the back, and transverse spinous muscles.

Attachments. -1°. To a common aponeurosis, to the posterior portion of the iliac crest, to the angles of the twelve ribs, to the transverse processes and vertebral laminæ, from the inferior portion of the sacrum, as far as the third cervical vertebra.

2°. To the angles of the ribs, to the transverse processes of four or five of the last cervical vertebra, also to those of the dorsal and lumbar vertebra, and to the spinous processes of all the vertebra.

13. Great oblique muscle. (*See* Pl. xii.)
14. Gluteus maximus. (*See* Pl. xix.)
15. Gluteus medius. (*See* Pl. xxi.)
16. Tensor of the aponeurosis of the limb. (*See* Pl. xxi.)

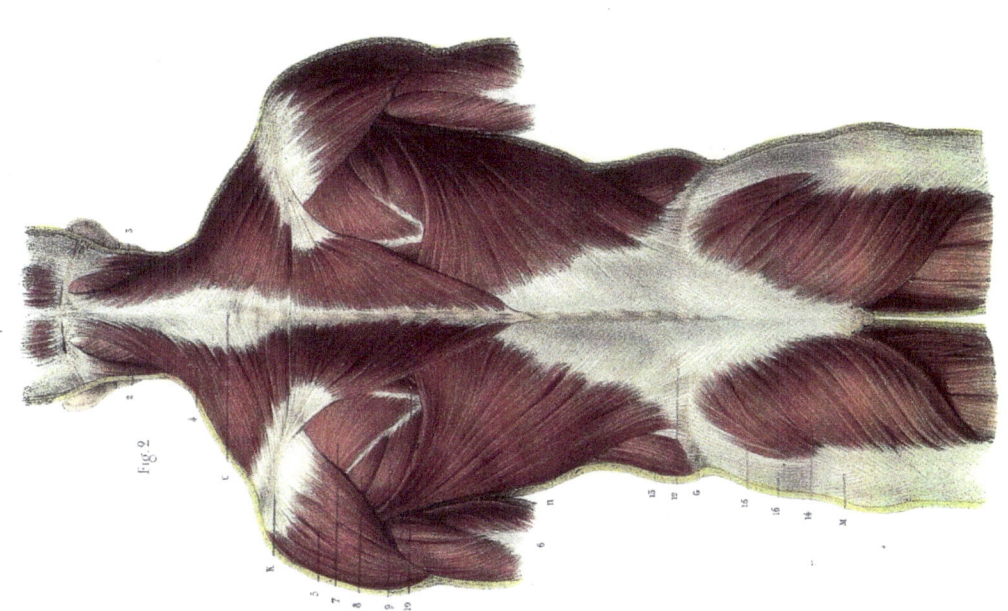

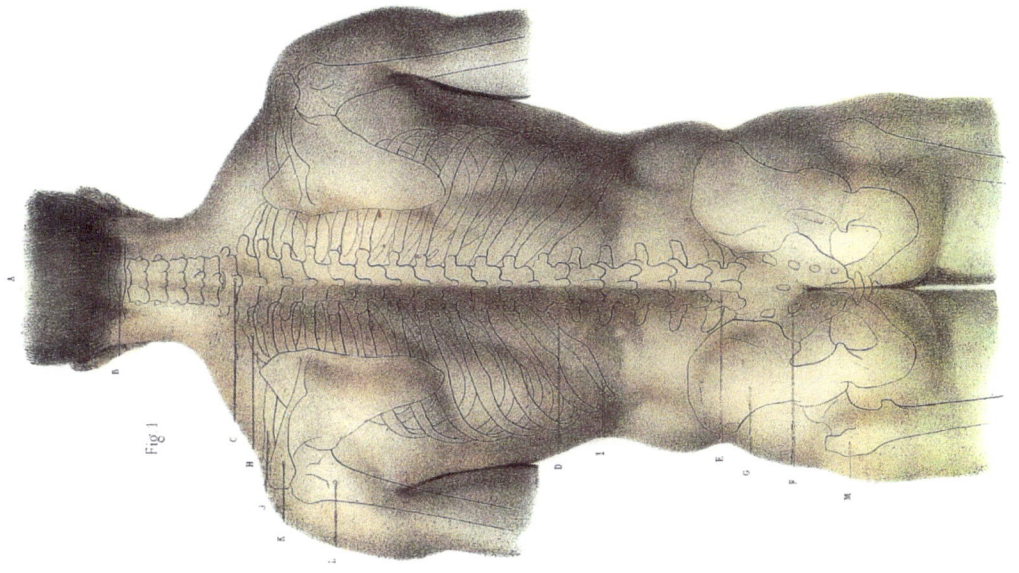

Paris
MÉQUIGNON MARVIS & GERMER BAILLIÈRE

PL 12

PLATE XIII.

FIGURE 1.

A. Seventh cervical vertebra.

B. Twelfth dorsal vertebra.

C. Fifth lumbar vertebra.

D. Sacrum and coccyx.

E. Coxal bone.

F. Collar bone.

G. Breast bone.

H. Seventh rib.

I. Scapula.

J. Humerus.

K. Femur.

L. Lingual bones.

FIGURE 2.

E. Iliac crest.

F. Collar bone.

I. Spine of the scapula.

K. Great trochanter.

L. Lingual bones.

1. Sterno-mastoid muscle. (*See* Pl. ix.)

2. Trapezius. (*See* Pl. xi.)

3. Splenius and levator of the angle of the scapula. (*See* Pl. ix.)

4. Scaleni muscles, anterior and posterior. (*See* Pl. ix.)

5. Sterno-hyoideus. *See* Pl. ix.)

6. Omo-hyoideus. (*See* Pl. ix.)

7. Digastricus. (*See* Pl. ix.)

8. Deltoid muscle.

Attachments.—1°. To the inferior edge of the spine of the scapula, to the external edge of the acromion, to the outer third of the anterior margin of the collar bone.

2°. To the deltoid impression of the humerus.

9. Great pectoral. *See* Pl. x.

10. Rectus of the abdomen, covered by its aponeurosis. (*See* Pl. x.)

11. Great oblique.

Attachments.—1°. To the anterior half of the iliac crest, and to the external edge of the anterior abdominal aponeurosis.

2°. To the outer surface and inferior margin of seven or eight of the lowermost ribs. The four or five uppermost digitations interlock with those of the serratus magnus, the remainder with those of the latissimus dorsi.

12. Serratus magnus.

Attachments.—1°. To the uppermost ribs.

2°. To all the outer edge of the scapula. The first digitation of the muscle is attached to the first two ribs, the remaining eight to the following ribs, from the third to the tenth inclusive, interlocking with the digitations of the great oblique muscle.

13. Great dorsal. (*See* Pl. xi.)

14. Gluteus maximus.

15. Gluteus medius.

16. Tensor of the aponeurosis.

17. Sartorius.

18. Rectus femoris, or cruris

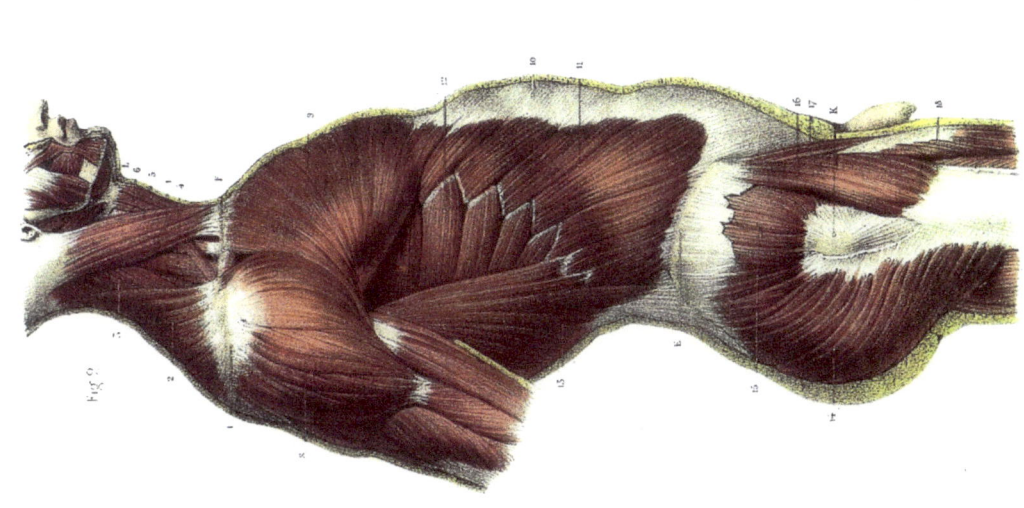

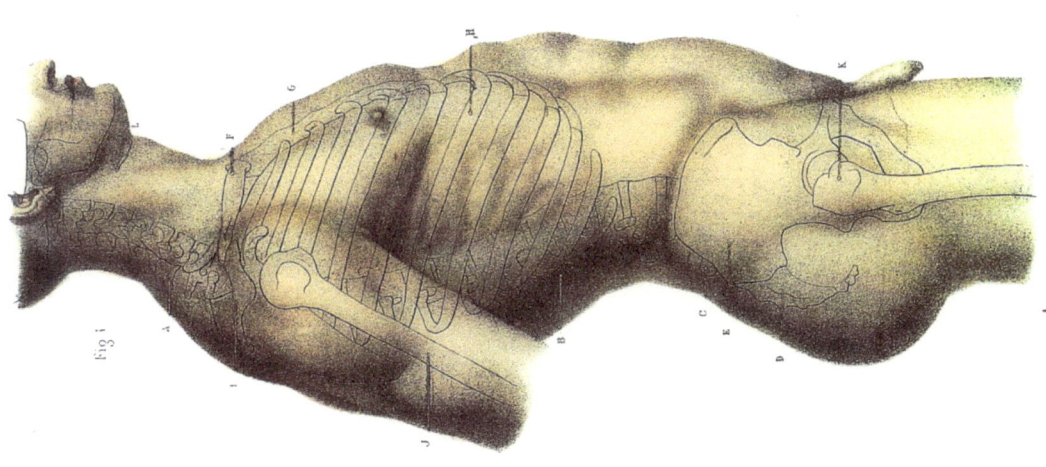

PL. 13

Fig. 2.

Fig. 1.

Paris
MÉQUIGNON-MARVIS._GERMER BAILLIÈRE

Imp. Lemercier, Paris.

Fau_2me Addition.

PLATE XIV.

FIGURE 1.

A. Collar bone.
B. Acromio-clavicular articulation.
C. Humerus.
D. Cubit.
E. Radius.
F. Bones of the carpus.
G. Bones of the metacarpus.
H. First phalanges.
I. Second phalanges.
K. Third phalanges.

FIGURE 2.

A. Collar bone.
B. Acromio-clavicular articulation.
C. Internal tuberosity (condyle) of the humerus.
D. Scaphoid bone.
E. Pisiform bone.
1. Great pectoral. (*See* Pl. x., Fig. 2.)
2. Trapezius. (*See* Pl. xi.)
3. Deltoid. (*See* Pl. xii.)
4. Biceps.

Attachments.—1°. The long portion is attached to the summit of the coracoid process by a tendon, common to it, with the coraco-brachialis muscle. The short portion, after passing through the bicipital groove, is attached to the upper margin of the glenoid cavity.

Note.—Anatomists usually call the latter, the long head of the biceps; and the former, the short head.

2°. To the posterior part of the bicipital tuberosity of the radius, and to the aponeurosis of the fore-arm by its aponeurotic expansion 4'. All these details are demonstrated in Figure 3 of the same plate.

5. Triceps. (*See* Pl. xiv.)
6. Anterior brachial, or brachialis flexor muscle.

Attachments.—1°. To the humerus, below the deltoid impression, to its internal and external aspects, and to its anterior internal and external edges.

2°. To the cubit, below the coronoid process.

7. Supinator longus. (*See* Pl. xv.)
8. First radial extensor. (*See* Pl. xv.)
9. Second radial extensor. (*See* Pl. xv.)
10. Pronator teres muscle: the rounded pronator.

Attachments.—1°. To the coronoid process of the cubit, to the inner condyle and inferior portion of the inner edge of the humerus, and to the aponeuroses.

2°. To the middle portion of the external surface of the radius.

11. Great palmar muscle: flexor radialis.

Attachments.—1°. To the inner condyle of the humerus, and to the aponeuroses.

2°. To the second metacarpal bone, and to the trapezium; sometimes to the third metacarpal.

12. Small palmar: palmaris longus muscle.

Attachments.—1°. The same as the preceding.
2°. To the anterior annular ligament of the carpus, and to the palmar aponeurosis 12'.

13. Common superficial flexor muscle. (*See* Pl. xvi.)
14. Anterior cubital: flexor carpi ulnaris.
15. Long proper flexor of the thumb.

Attachments.—1°. To the three upper fourths of the radius, to the adjoining portion of the interosseous ligament, and to the anterior margin of the bone.

2°. To the anterior portion of the upper end of the last phalanx of the thumb.

16. The square-formed pronator.

Attachments.—1°. To the lower fourth of the inner edge, and to the anterior surface of the cubit.

2°. To the inferior fourth of the external margin of the inner margin, and anterior aspect of the radius.

17. Annular ligament of the carpus.
18. Short abductor of the thumb.

Attachments.—1°. To the annular ligament, to the scaphoid, and frequently to an aponeurotic expansion of the long abductor.

2°. To the external portion of the superior extremity of the first phalanx of the thumb.

19. Palmaris brevis; cutaneous palmar muscle.

Attachments.—1°. To the inner margin of the palmar aponeurosis, to the anterior annular ligament of the carpus.

2°. To the skin.

20. Sheaths of the tendons.

52

FIGURE 3.

A. Bicipital groove of the humerus.

A'. Internal tuberosity, or condyle of the same bone.

B. Coracoid process.

C. Cubit.

D. Radius.

1. Fleshy body of the biceps muscle.

2. Tendon of the short portion penetrating into the bicipital groove.

3. Tendon of the long portion, attached to the coracoid process.

4. Inferior tendon fixed to the bicipital tuberosity of the radius.

5. Aponeurotic expansion cut across to expose the cubital attachment of the brachialis flexor.

6. Coraco-brachialis.

Attachments.—1°. To the coracoid process with the long portion of the biceps.

2°. To the margin and inner aspect of the humerus towards its middle portion.

7. 7. Triceps brachii; an extensor muscle.

8. 8. Anterior brachial; a flexor.

9. Its inferior attachment under the coronoid process of the ulna.

10. Tendon of the great pectoral, cut across.

11. Deltoid, also cut across.

FIGURE 4.

1. Palmaris longus or gracilis, cut across. The palmar aponeurosis has been removed in order to expose the muscles of the hand.

2. Adductor of the little finger.

Attachments.—1°. To the pisiform bone.

2°. To the inner side of the first phalanx of the little finger.

3. Short flexor of the thumb.

Attachments.—1°. To the trapezium, to the annular ligament and os magnum.

2°. To the external sesamoid bone of the joint, and to the first phalanx of the thumb.

3. Opposing muscle of the thumb. (*See* Pl. xv.)

4. Short flexor of the little finger.

Attachments.—1°. To the hook-shaped bone, and to the annular ligament.

2°. To the inner side of the first phalanx of the little finger.

7. First dorsal inter-osseous. (*See* Pl. xiv.)

8. First lumbricalis. These small muscles, three in number, are merely accessories of the flexors.

9. A fibrous sheath laid open to show the arrangement of the tendons.

53

PL. 14

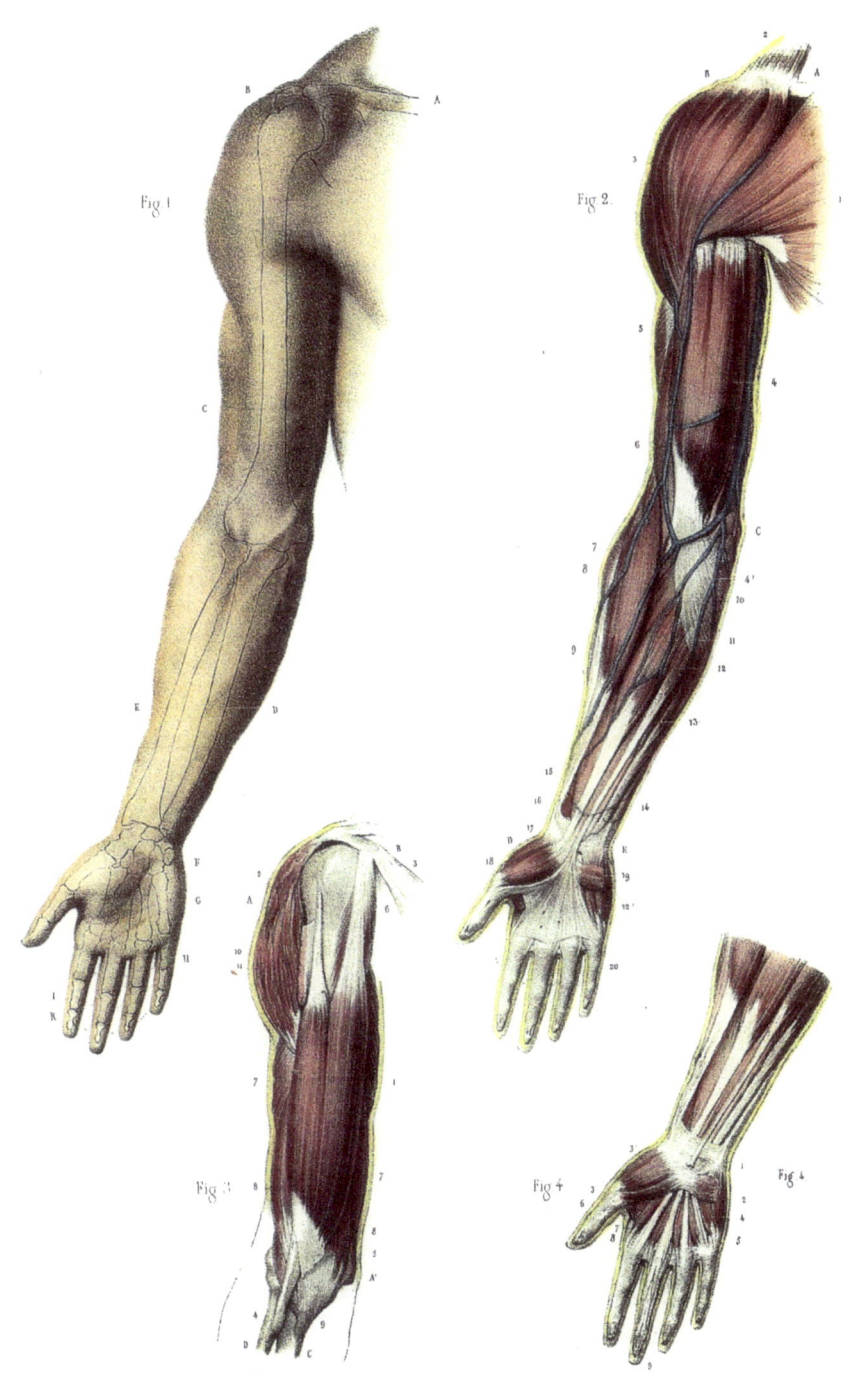

Fig 1.

Fig 2.

Fig 3

Fig 4

Fau 2.me édition

Paris

Imp. Lemercier, Paris

MÉQUIGNON MARVIS   GERMER BAILLIÈRE

54

PLATE XV.

FIGURE 1.

A. Spine of the scapula and acromion process.
B. Humerus.
C. Cubit.
D. Radius.
E. Carpus.
F. Metacarpus.
G. First phalanges.
H. Second phalanges.
I. Third phalanges.

FIGURE 2.

A. Acromion.
B. Inner condyle of the humerus.
C. Olecranon.
D. Lower end of the cubit.
E. Lower end of the radius.
1. The whole of the muscles of the scapula. (*See* Pl. xi., Fig 2.)
2. Trapezius muscle. (*See* Pl. xi., Fig. 2.)
3. Deltoid. (*See* Pl. xii.)
4. Triceps.

Attachments.—1°. By its long portion to the axillary margin of the scapula, near the glenoid cavity. By its external portion to the posterior surface of the humerus above the osseous groove, and to the external aspect of the bone. By its inner portion to the posterior surface of the bone, and to its inner edge below the osseous groove.
2°. To the upper and back part of the olecranon.

4. Common tendon of the triceps. (*See* Fig. 3.)
5. Brachialis flexor. (*See* Pl. xiii.)
6. Long supinator. (*See* Pl. xv.)
7. First, or long radial extensor. (*See* Pl. xv.)
8. Anconeus muscle.

Attachments.—1°. To the posterior part of the external condyle of the humerus.
2°. To the triangular surface of the posterior aspect of the cubit.

9. Anterior cubital muscle, or flexor carpi ulnaris.

Attachments.—1°. To the inner condyle of the humerus, to the inner margin of the olecranon, and to the aponeuroses.
2°. To the pisiform bone, and to the fifth metacarpal.

10. Second radial extensor. (*See* Pl. xv.)
11. Common extensor of the fingers.

Attachments.—1°. To the external condyle of the humerus, and to the aponeuroses.
2°. To the second and third phalanges of the four last fingers. (*See* Fig. 4.)

12. Extensor proprius of the little finger.

Attachments.—1°. To the outer condyle of the humerus, and the aponeuroses.
2°. To the fourth tendon of the common extensor.

13. Posterior cubital muscle.

Attachments.—1°. To the external condyle of the humerus, and to the posterior surface and posterior edge of the cubit.
2°. To the upper end of the fifth metacarpal bone.

14. Short extensor of the thumb. (*See* Pl. xv.)
14'. Long abductor of the thumb. (*See* Pl. xv.)
15. Annular ligament of the carpus.
16. Tendon of the long extensor of the thumb.

Attachments.—1°. To the cubit, to the interosseous ligament, and to the aponeuroses.
2°. To the upper end of the last phalanx of the thumb.

17. Fibrous sheaths of the tendons.

FIGURE 3.

A. Acromion process.
B. Humerus.
B'. Inner condyle of the humerus.
C. Ulna or cubit.
D. Radius.
1. External portion of the triceps.
1. Its superior attachment.
2. Middle or long portion of the same muscle.
3. Superior fasciculus.
2' and 3'. Superior attachments.
4. Inner portion and common tendon of the muscle.

FIGURE 4.

A. Radius.
B. Cubit.
1. Tendon of the short radial extensor.
2. Tendon of the long radial extensor.
3. Tendon of the extensor brevis of the thumb.
4. First dorsal inter-osseous muscle.

Attachments.—1°. To the inner margin of the first metacarpal bone, and to the external surface of the second.
2°. To the outer side of the first phalanx of the index.

5. Adductor of the thumb. (*See* Pl. xiii.)
6. Opponens and adductor of the thumb. (*See* Pl. xiii. and xvi.)
7. Tendons of the extensors.
8. Little uniting tendinous bands.

Pl. 15

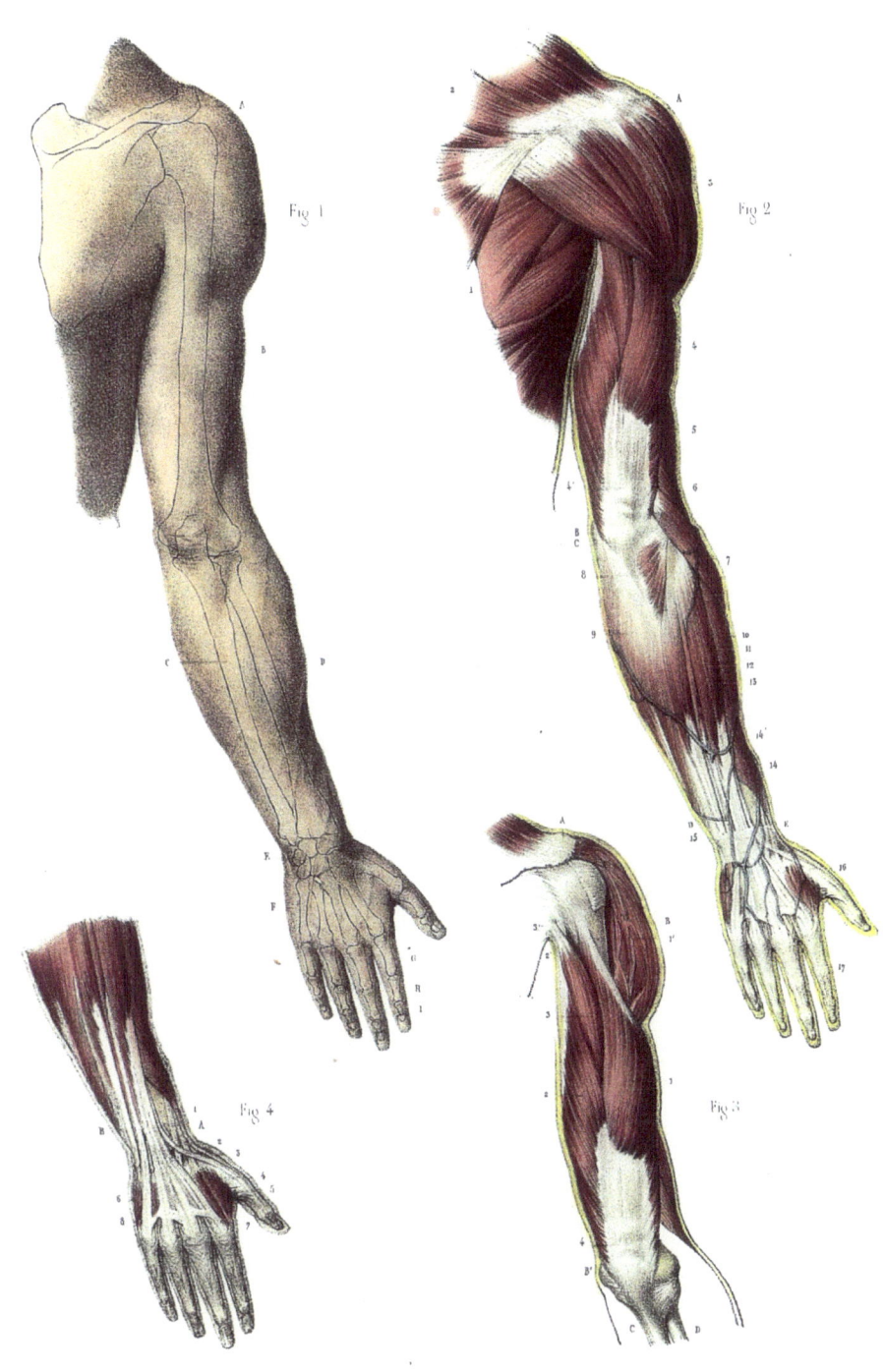

Fig 1

Fig 2

Fig 4

Fig 3

Fau 9.me edition   Paris   Imp Lemercier, Paris

MÉQUIGNON MARVIS   GERMER BAILLIÈRE.

PLATE XVI.

FIGURE 1.

A. Scapula.
B. Collar bone.
C. Humerus.
D. Ulna.
E. Radius.
F. Carpus.
G. Metacarpus.
H. First phalanges.
I. Second phalanges.
J. Third phalanges.

FIGURE 2.

A. Scapula.
B. Collar bone.
C. Olecranon process.
D. Radius.
1. Trapezius muscle. (*See* Pl. xi.)
2. Great pectoral. (*See* Pl. x.)
3. Deltoid. (*See* Pl. xii.)
4. Muscles of the scapula. (*See* Pl. xi.)
5. Biceps. (*See* Pl. xiii.)
6. Brachialis flexor. (*See* Pl. xiii.)
7. Triceps. (*See* Pl. xiv.)
8. Long supinator.

Attachments.—1°. To the lower third of the external margin of the humerus.

2°. To the base of the styloid process of the radius.

9. Great palmar muscle, or flexor carpi radialis. (*See* Pl. xiii.)

10. First external radial muscle, or extensor carpi radialis longior.

Attachments.—1°. To the external condyle of the humerus, and to the upper part of the external edge of the humerus, and to a tendon common to it with the muscles of the posterior region of the fore arm.

2°. To the back part of the upper extremity of the second metacarpal bone.

11. Second external radial muscle.

Attachments.—1°. To the outer condyle of the humerus by the common tendon, and to the aponeuroses.

2°. To the upper end of the third metacarpal bone. For the inferior insertions of these muscles, *see* Pl. xiv. Fig. 4.

12. Anconeus muscle. (*See* Pl. xiv.)

13. Long common extensor of the fingers. (*See* Pl. xiv.)

14. Proper extensor of the little finger. (*See* Pl. xiv.)

15. Posterior ulnar muscle. (*See* Pl. xiv.)

16. Long abductor of the thumb.

Attachments.—1°. To the ulna, the radius, the inter-osseous ligament, and to an aponeurosis.

2°. To the upper end of the metacarpal bone.

17. Short extensor of the thumb.

Attachments.—1°. To the ulna, to the radius, and to the inter-osseous ligament.

2°. To the upper end of the first phalanx of the thumb.

18. Ligament of the carpus.

19. Tendon of the long extensor of the thumb. (*See* Pl. xiv.)

20. Opposing muscle of the thumb.

Attachments.—1°. To the trapezium, and to the anterior annular ligament of the carpus.

2°. To the outer edge of the first metacarpal bone.

21. First dorsal inter-osseal muscle. (*See* Pl. xiv.)
22. Abductor of the thumb. (*See* Pl. xiii.)

FIGURE 3.

A. Humerus.
B. Olecranon process of the ulna.
C. The radius.
D. The carpus.
E. The metacarpus.

FIGURE 4.

A. The olecranon.
B. Lower end of the ulna.
1. Deltoid muscle.
2. Biceps.
3. Brachialis flexor.
4. External portion of the triceps.
5. Long supinator.
6. First radial extensor.
7. Second radial extensor.
8. Long common extensor of the fingers.
9. Proper extensor of the little finger.
10. Posterior or cubital extensor.
11. Anconeus muscle.
12. Anterior or flexor cubital muscle.
13. Long abductor and short extensor of the thumb.
14. Abductor of the little finger.
15. Cutaneous or short palmar muscle, cut across.
16. Annular ligament of the carpus.

Pl. 16

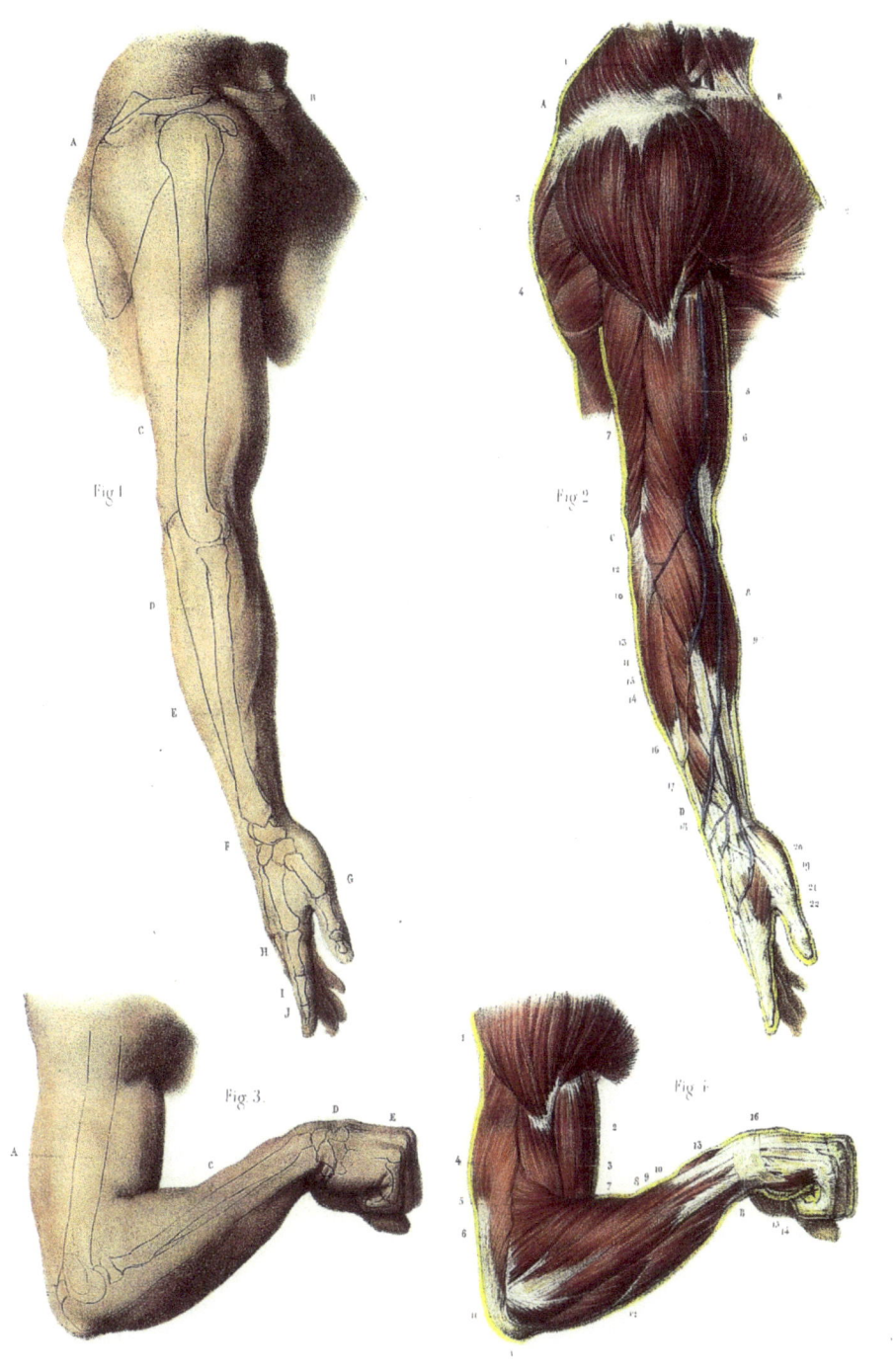

Fig 1.

Fig 2.

Fig 3.

Fig 4.

Paris 2ᵐᵉ edition

Paris

Imp.Lemercier a Paris.

MÉQUIGNON MARVIS   GERMER BAILLIÈRE

PLATE XVII.

FIGURE 1.

A. Collar bone.
B. Humerus.
C. The cubit.
D. Radius.
E. Carpus.
F. Metacarpus.
G. First phalanges.
H. Second phalanges.
I. Third phalanges.

FIGURE 2.

A. Acromio-clavicular articulation.
B. Inner condyle of the humerus.
C. Olecranon process.
D. Lower end of the ulna.
E. Pisiform bone.
1. Deltoid. (See Pl. xii.)
2. Great pectoral. (See Pl. x.)
3. Biceps. (See Pl. xiii.)
3'. Its aponeurotic expansion.
4. Brachialis flexor muscle. (See Pl. xiii.)
5. Coraco-brachialis muscle. (See Pl. xiii., Fig. 3.)
6. Outer portion of the triceps. (See Pl. xiv.)
7. Long supinator. (See Pl. xv.)
8. The round pronator. (See Pl. xiii.)
9. The great palmar, or flexor carpi radialis. (See Pl. xiii.)
10. Palmaris longis. (See Pl. xii.)
11. Superficial flexor of the fingers.

Attachments.—1°. To the inner condyle of the humerus by the common tendon of the superficial muscles, to the coronoid process of the ulna, to the anterior margin of the radius, to the aponeuroses.

2°. To the second phalanges of the four last fingers.

12. Flexor carpi ulnaris. (See Pl. xiv.)
13. Ligament of the carpus.
14. Adductor of the little finger. (See Pl. xiii.

15. Section of the cutaneous palma. (See Pl. xiii.)
16. Short abductor of the thumb. (See Pl. xiii.)

FIGURE 3.

A. Humerus.
B. Olecranon.
C. Radius.
D. Carpus.
E. Metacarpus.

FIGURE 4.

A. Inner tuberosity of the humerus. (Condyle.)
B. Olecranon.
C. Lower end of the radius.
1. Deltoid muscle.
2. Extremity of the great pectoral muscle.
3. Biceps.
3'. Its aponeurotic expansion.
4. Brachialis flexor.
5. Coraco-brachialis.
6. Triceps.
7. Long supinator.
8. Round pronator.
9. Flexor C. radialis.
10. Palmaris longus.
11. Superficial flexor of the fingers.
12. Flexor carpi ulnaris.
13. Ligament of the carpus.
14. Long abductor of the thumb.
15. Short extensor of the thumb.
16. Long extensor of the thumb.
17. First dorsal inter-osseons.
18. Opponens of the thumb.
19. Abductor of the thumb.

Note.—In Copying Figure 2, the student may as well omit the superficial veins; the aponeurosis, which has been removed, lays between these veins and the muscles.

Pl. 17

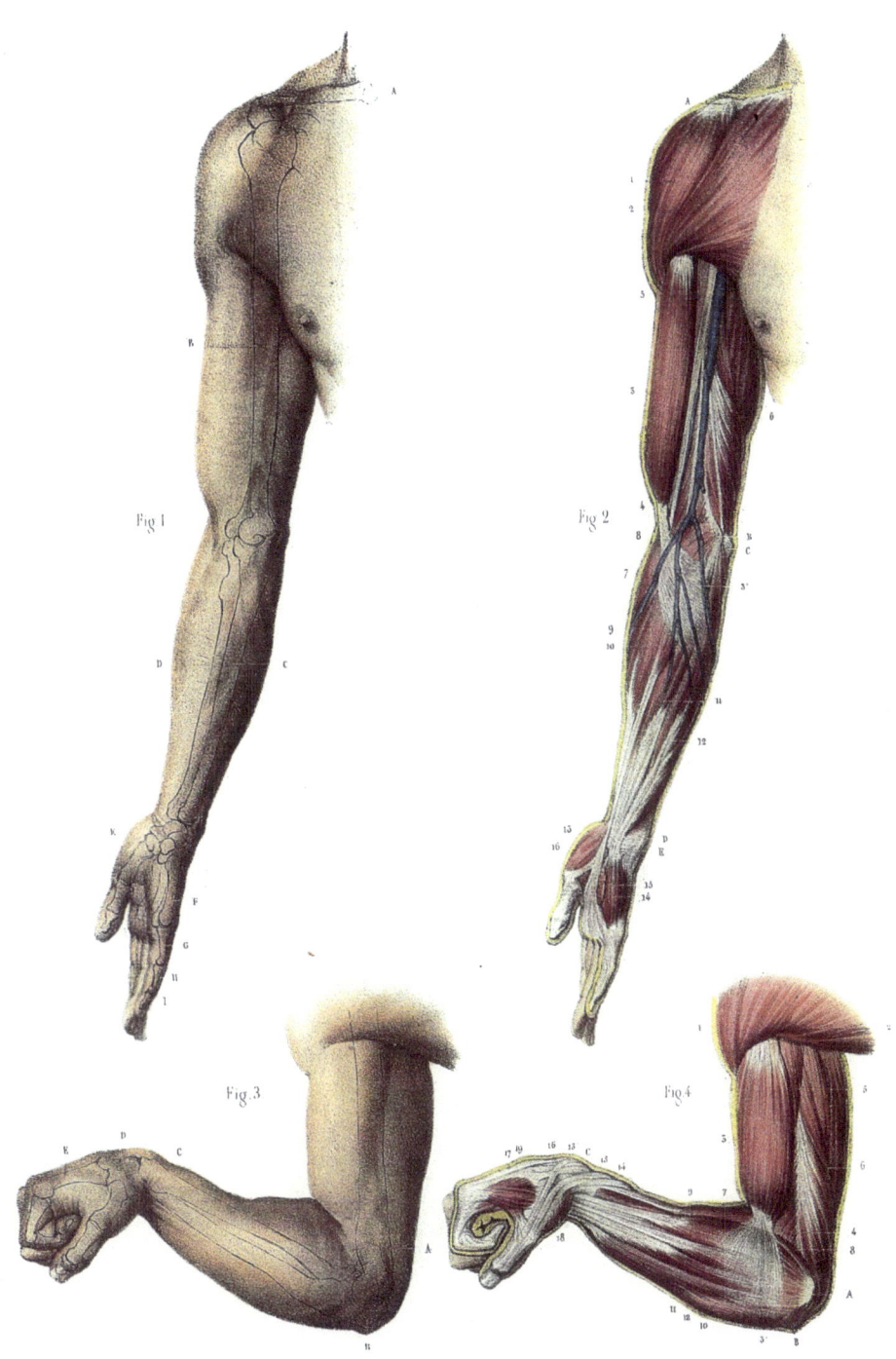

Fig 1

Fig 2

Fig. 3

Fig. 4

Fau 2me edition

Paris

Imp Lemercier Paris

MÉQUIGNON MARVIS   GERMER BAILLIÈRE

60

PLATE XVIII.

FIGURE 1.

A. The ulna.
B. The radius.
C. The humerus.
D. The scapula.
E. The collar bone.

FIGURE 2.

A. The ulna.
B. The radius.
C. The humerus.
1. Flexor ulnaris.
2. Superficial common flexor.
3. Long palmar.
4. Great palmar, flexor radialis.
5. Long supinator.
6. Biceps.
6'. Its aponeurotic expansion.
7. Brachialis flexor.
8. Triceps.
8'. Its inferior tendon.
9. Coraco-brachialis.
10. Great pectoral.
11. and 11*. Deltoid.
12. Teres major,
13. Sub-scapular.
14. Latissimus dorsi.
15. Serratus magnus.

FIGURE 3.

A. Cubit.
B. Radius.
C. Humerus.
D. Scapula.
E. Collar bone.

FIGURE 4.

D. Spine of the scapula.
1. Anconeus muscle.
2. Anterior cubital.
3. Posterior cubital.
4. Proper extensor of the little finger.
5. Common extensor of the fingers.
6. Short extensor of the thumb.
7. Long abductor of the thumb.
8. 2° Radialis externus.
9. 1° Radialis externus.
10. The long supinator.
11. Brachialis flexor.
12. Biceps.
13. Triceps.
13'. Its inferior tendon.
14. Deltoid.
15. Latissimus dorsi.
16. Teres major.
17. Teres minor.
18. Infra spinatus.
19. Rhomboideus.
20. Trapezius, of which a portion has been removed to show the position and action of the supra-spinatus muscle.

Pl. 18

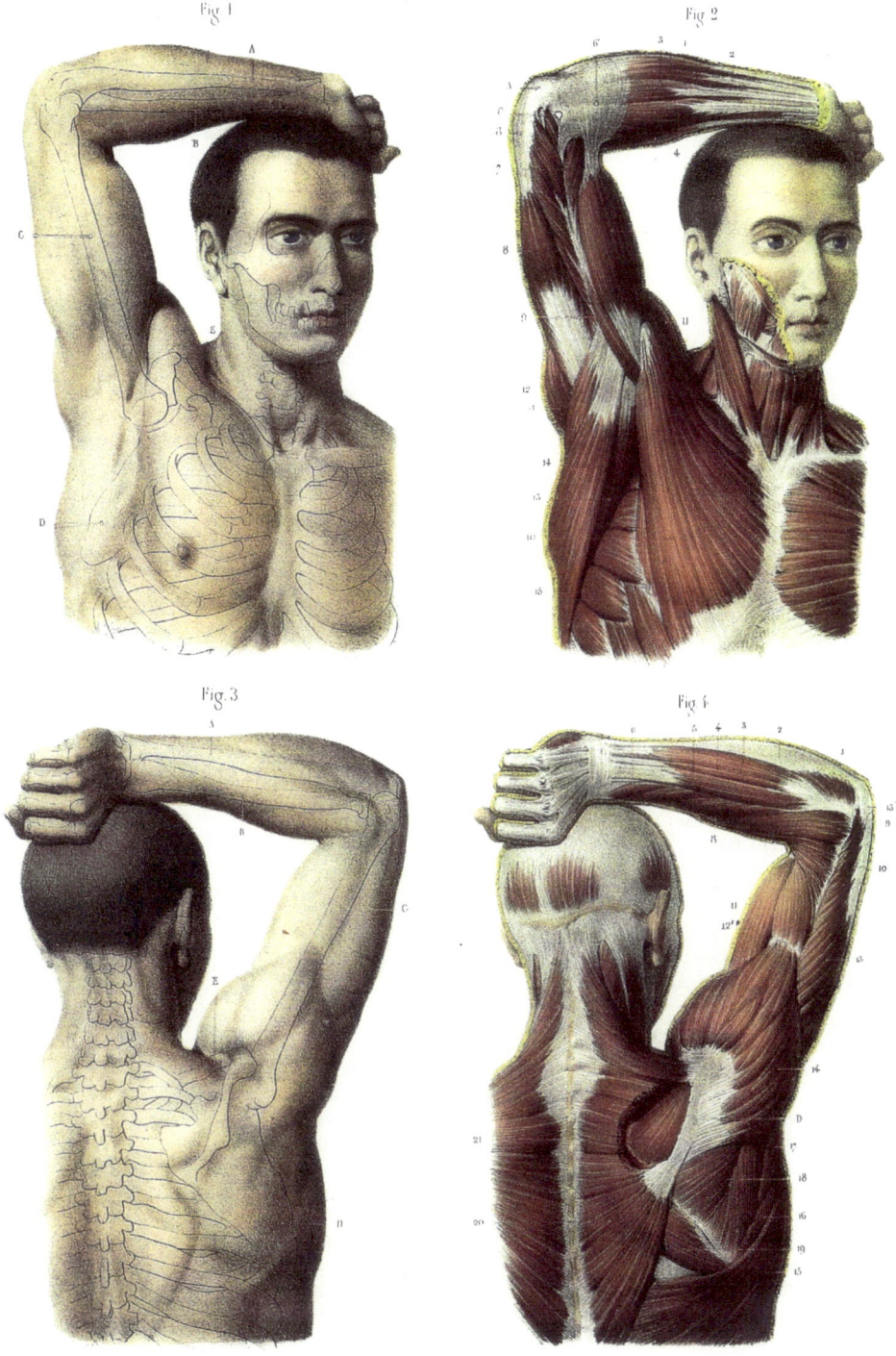

Fig. 1
Fig. 2
Fig. 3
Fig. 4

Fau 2me édition
Paris
Imp Lemercier Paris
MÉQUIGNON MARVIS   GERMER BAILLIÈRE

PLATE XIX.

FIGURE 1.

A. Coxal bone.
B. Femur.
C. Rotula.
D. Tibia.
E. Fibula.
F. Tarsus.
G. Metatarsus.
H. Phalanges.

FIGURE 2.

A. Anterior and superior iliac spine.
B. Inner condyle of the femur.
C. Rotula.
D. Tuberosity of the tibia.
E. Head of the fibula.
1. Psoas muscle.

Attachments.—1°. To the lateral portions of the bodies, and of the inter-vertebral substances of the twelfth dorsal vertebra, and of the five lumbar, to the base of their transverse processes.

2°. To the smaller trochanter.

2. Iliac muscle.

Attachments.—1°. To the iliac fossa and crest, to the base of the sacrum, to the capsule of the hip joint, and to a ligament.

2°. To the smaller trochanter, with the preceding muscle.

3. Gluteus medius. (*See* Pl. xxi.)
4. Tensor of the fascia. (*See* Pl. xxi.)
5. Sartorius. (*See* Pl. xx.)
6. Rectus cruris.

Attachments.—1°. To the anterior and inferior iliac spine, and to the bone above the cotyloid cavity.

2°. To the superior edge of the rotula.

7. Triceps.

(This muscle forms, with the preceding, a true triceps muscle, omitting the central portion called crureus, and viewing it as really appertaining to the vasti, which I shall now describe.)

Attachments of the vasti.—1°. To the base of the great trochanter, and to the bone anterior to this eminence, to the oblique line running from the trochanter to the linea aspera, to the whole of the linea aspera, to the tendon of the gluteus maximus (this is the vastus externus); to an oblique line running from the neck of the femur to the linea aspera, to the outer, inner and anterior surfaces of the femur, and to its lateral margins (vastus internus).

2°. To the superior and lateral margins of the rotula, and to the aponeuroses around the knee.

8. Third adductor. (*See* Pl. xx.)
9. Gracilis. (*See* Pl. xx.)
10. First adductor.

Attachments.—1°. To the spine of the pubis, and to a portion of the bone below the spine.

2°. To the middle of the linea aspera.

11. Pectineus.

Attachments.—1°. To the spine and crest of the pubis, and to the bone before the crest.

2°. To the line running from the small trochanter to the linea aspera.

12. Tibialis anticus.

Attachments.—1°. To the external tuberosity of the tibia, to the oblique line of the anterior tuberosity, to the three upper fourths of the external surface of the bone, to the inter-osseous ligament.

2°. To the tubercle of the first cuneiform bone, and to the first metatarsal.

13. Long common extensor. (*See* Pl. xxi.)
14. Long extensor of the great toe.

Attachments.—1°. To the inner surface of the fibula, and somewhat to the inter-osseous ligament behind the preceding.

2°. To the posterior extremity of the second phalanx of the great toe.

15. Anterior peroneus. (*See* Pl. xxi.)
16. Peroneus longus. (*See* Pl. xx.)
17. Soleus muscle. (*See* Pl. xix.)
18. Gastro-cnemius internus. (*See* Pl. xix.)
19. Soleus. (*See* Pl. xix.)
20. Long common flexor of the toes. (*See* Pl. xx.)
21. Pediosus, or short common extensor. (*See* Pl. xxi.)
22. Adductor of the great toe. (*See* Pl. xx.)
23. Annular ligament of the tarsus.

FIGURE 3.

A. Coxal bone.
B. Head of the femur in its capsule.
C. Rotula.
1. 1. Superior and inferior extremities of the rectus, or anterior portion of the triceps.
2. Interior portion of the psoas and iliac muscles.
3. 3. Internal and external portions of the triceps — the vasti.
4. Gluteus medius.
5. Gluteus minimus.
6. Pectineus.
7. First adductor, or adductor longus.
8. Second adductor, or adductor brevis.

63

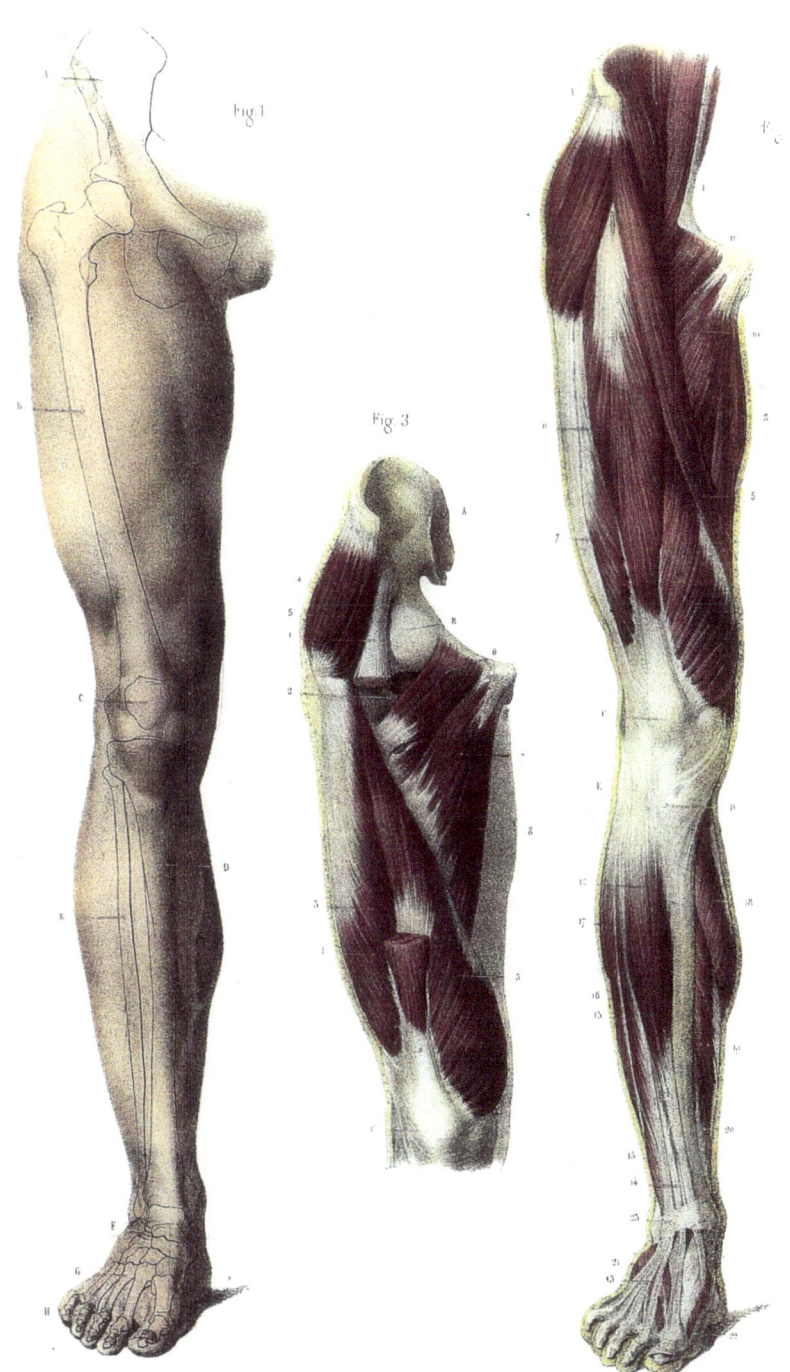

Fig.1

Fig.3

rau _ 2ᵐᵉ édition

Paris
MÉQUIGNON MARVIS _ GERMER-BAILLÈRE.

Imp Lemercier et Cᵢᵉ Paris

PLATE XX.

FIGURE 1.

A. Sacrum and coccyx.
B. Iliac bone.
C. Femur.
D. Tibia.
E. Fibula.
F. Astragalus.
G. Calcaneum.
H. Metatarsus and phalanges.

FIGURE 2.

B. Iliac bone.
C. Great trochanter.
D. Malleolus internus.
E. Malleolus externus.
G. Calcaneum.
1. Gluteus medius. (*See* Pl. xxi.)
2. Tensor fasciæ latæ. (*See* Pl. xx.)
3. Gluteus maximus.

Attachments.—1°. To the upper curved line of the iliac bone as far as the crest, to the crest of the sacrum, to the lateral margins of this bone and of the coccyx, to ligaments, and to the aponeurosis of the thigh.

2°. To the rugosities of the femur, extending from the great trochanter to the linea aspera.

4. Triceps. (*See* Pl. xviii.)
5. Biceps.

Attachments —1°. To the sciatic tuberosity by its long portion, to the linea aspera of the femur by its short portion.

6. Semi-tendinosus.

Attachments.—1°. To the sciatic tuberosity with the preceding.
2°. To the anterior tuberosity of the tibia.

7. Semi-membranosus.

Attachments.—1°. With the preceding muscles.

2°. To the inner tuberosity of the tibia, and below the external condyle of the femur.
8. Third adductor. (*See* Pl. xx.)
9. Gracilis. (*See* Pl. xx.)
10. Sartorius. (*See* Pl. xx.)
11 and 11′. Gastro-cnemii muscles and tendo-achilles.

Attachments.—1°. To the rough impressions of the femur above the condyles.
2°. To the calcaneum by the tendo-achilles.

12. Plantaris—its tendon.

Attachments.—1°. Above the external condyle of the femur, and to the fibrous capsule of the joint.
2°. To the calcaneum.

13. Soleus muscle.

Attachments.—1°. To the back part of the head of the fibula, to the outer edge of the posterior surface of the bone, to the middle portion of the inner edge of the tibia, to the aponeuroses.
2°. To the calcaneum by the tendo-achilles.

14. Long common flexor muscle of the toes. (*See* Pl. xx.)
15. Tendon of the tibialis posticus. (*See* Pl. xx.)
16. Peroneus longus. (*See* Pl. xxi)
17. Peroneus brevis (*See* Pl. xxi)

Pl. 20

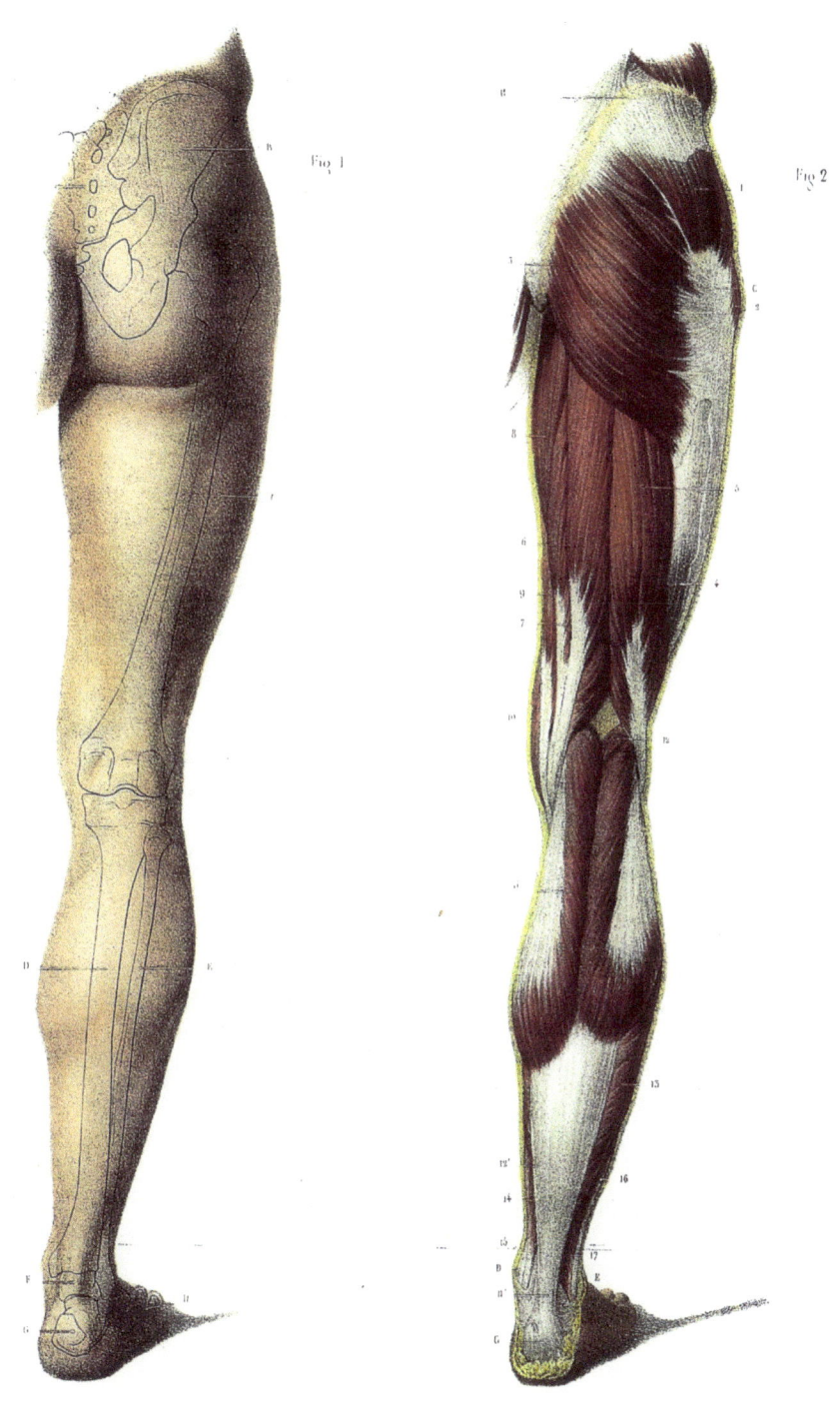

Fig 1

Fig 2

Eau 2me edition   Paris   Imp Lemercier, a Paris

MÉQUIGNON MARVIS   GERMER BAILLIÈRE

PLATE XXI.

FIGURE 1.

A. Coxal bone.
B. Femur.
C. Rotula.
D. Tibia.
E. Fibula.
F. Tarsus.
G. Metatarsus.
H. Phalanges.

FIGURE 2.

A. Anterior and superior iliac spine.
A'. Articular surface of the pubis.
a. Sacrum and coccyx.
B. Internal tuberosity of the femur.
C. Rotula.
D. Tibia.
1. Psoas muscle. (*See* Pl. xviii.)
2. Iliac muscle. (*See* Pl. xviii.)
3. Gluteus maximus. (*See* Pl. xix.)
4. Sartorius.

Attachments.—1°. To the anterior and superior iliac spine, and to the notch separating it from the inferior spine to the aponeurosis.

2°. To the inner part of the crest of the tibia, below the anterior tuberosity.

5. Rectus extensor. (*See* Pl. xviii.)
6. Triceps. (*See* Pl. xviii.)
7. Pectineus. (*See* Pl. xviii.)
8. First adductor. (*See* Pl. xviii.)

9. Gracilis.

Attachments.—1°. To the pubis and its descending ramus.

2°. To the anterior tuberosity of the tibia, below the semi-tendinosus.

10. Third adductor.

Attachments.—1°. To the tuberosity of the ischion, to the ascending branch of that bone, and to the descending branch of the pubis.

2°. To the linea aspera of the femur, as far as the inner condyle.

11. Semi-membranosus. (*See* Pl. xix.)
12. Semi-tendinosus. (*See* Pl. xix.)
13 and 18'. Gastro-cnemius and tendon of achilles, tendon of the plantaris.
14. Soleus muscle. (*See* Pl. xix.)
15. Long common flexor muscle of the toes.

Attachments.—1°. To the oblique line of the tibia and to the middle portion of its posterior surface, to the aponeurosis.

2°. To the last phalanges of the four last toes.

16 and 17. Tendons of the tibialis posticus, and of the long flexor of the great toe.

18. Tibialis anticus. (*See* Pl. xviii.)
19. Short adductor of the great toe.

Attachments.—1°. To the calcaneum, to the inner annular ligament, to the plantar aponeurosis.

2°. To the inner part of the first phalanx of the great toe.

20. Annular ligament of the tarsus.

PL. 21.

Fig 1   Fig. 2

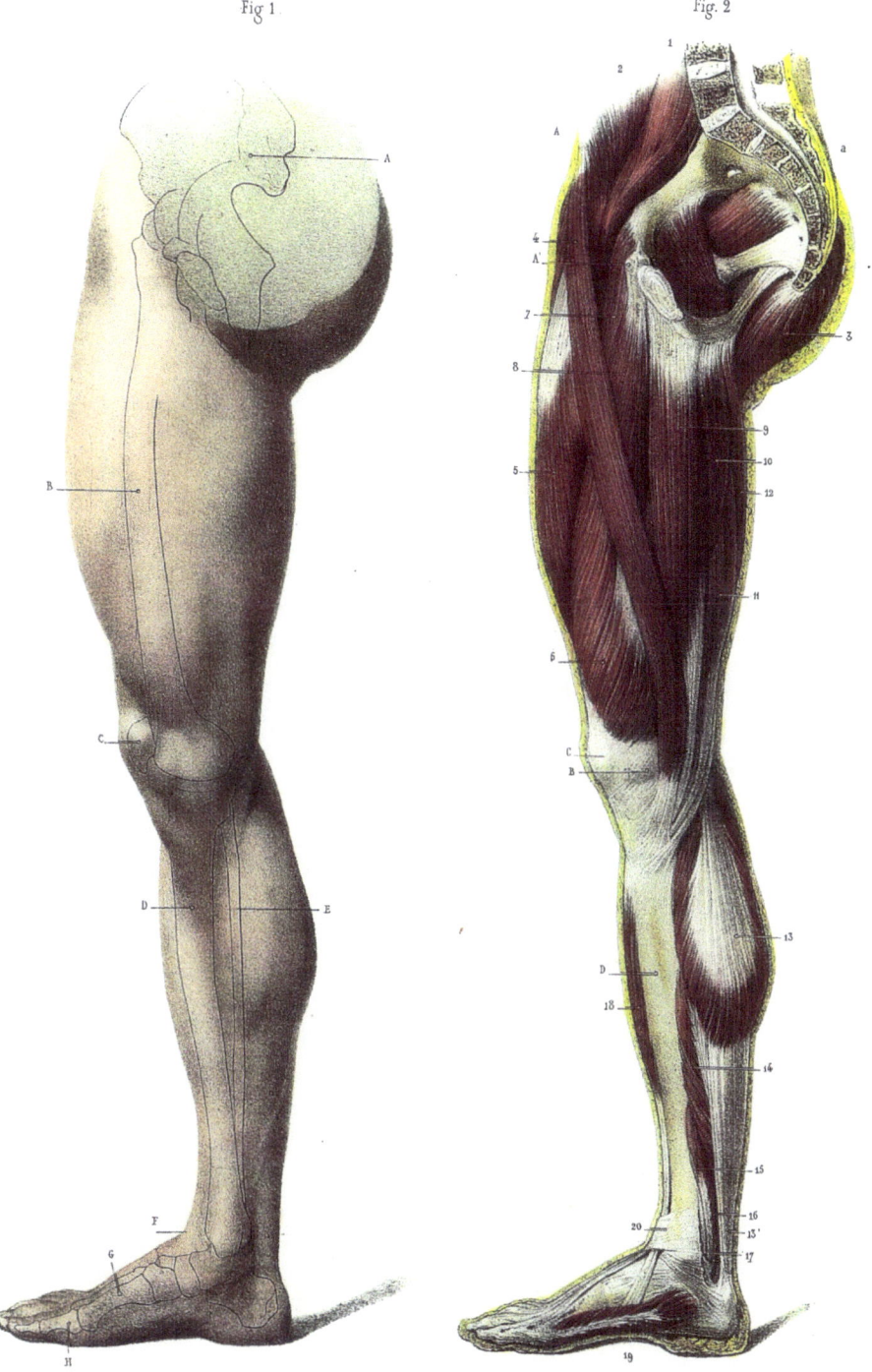

Fau_2^{me}édition   Paris   Imp. Lemercier & Cie Paris

MÉQUIGNON-MARVIS __GERMER BAILLÈRE

PLATE XXII.

FIGURE 1.

A. Iliac bone.
B. Sacrum and coccyx.
C. Femur.
D. Rotula.
E. Tibia.
F. Perone.
G. Tarsus.
H. Metatarsus.
I. Phalanges.

FIGURE 2.

A. Iliac crest.
C. Great trochanter.
D. Rotula.
E. External tuberosity of the tibia.
F. Head of the fibula.

1 and 1'. Tensor muscle of the aponeurosis of the thigh, strong aponeurotic band extending to the fibula.

Attachments.—1°. To the anterior portion of the external margin of the iliac crest, and to its anterior and superior spine.

2°. To the aponeurosis called fascia lata, which is itself attached to the external part of the anterior tuberosity of the tibia.

2. Gluteus medius.

Attachments.—1°. To the coxal bones, between the curved lines, and to the iliac crest, to the anterior and superior spine, and to the notch separating it from the inferior, to the aponeurosis, fascia lata.

2°. To the external aspect of the great trochanter.

3. Gluteus maximus. (*See* Pl. xix.)
4. Sartorius. (*See* Pl. xx.)
5. Rectus.
6. Triceps. (*See* Pl. xviii.)
7. Biceps. (*See* Pl. xix.)
8. Tibialis anticus. (*See* Pl. xviii.)

9. Gastro-cnemii. (*See* Pl. xix.)
10 and 10'. Soleus and tendo-achilles. (*See* Pl. xix.)
11. Peroneus longus.

Attachments.—1°. To the external tuberosity of the tibia, to the outer surface of the head of the fibula, to the anterior and posterior margins, and outer surface of that bone.

2°. To the posterior extremity of the first metatarsal bone.

12. Peroneus brevis.

Attachments.—1°. To the anterior and posterior margins, to the inferior part of the outer surface of the fibula, and to the aponeuroses.

13. Peroneus tertius, or anterior.

Attachments.—1°. To the lower portion of the inner surface of the fibula, to the inter-osseous ligament, and to the aponeuroses.

2°. To the posterior extremity of the fifth metatarsal bone.

14 and 14'. Long common extensor of the toes and its tendons.

Attachments.—1°. To the external tuberosity of the tibia, to the anterior half of the inner surface of the fibula, and to the inter-osseous ligament.

2°. To the second and third phalanges of the four last toes.

15. Pediosus.

Attachments.—1°. To the calcaneum.
2°. To the four first toes.

16. Abductor of the little toe.

Attachments.—1°. To the calcaneum, to the posterior extremity of the fifth metatarsal bone.

2°. To the posterior extremity of the little toe.

17. Annular ligament of the tarsus.

69

PL.22

Fig.1   Fig.2

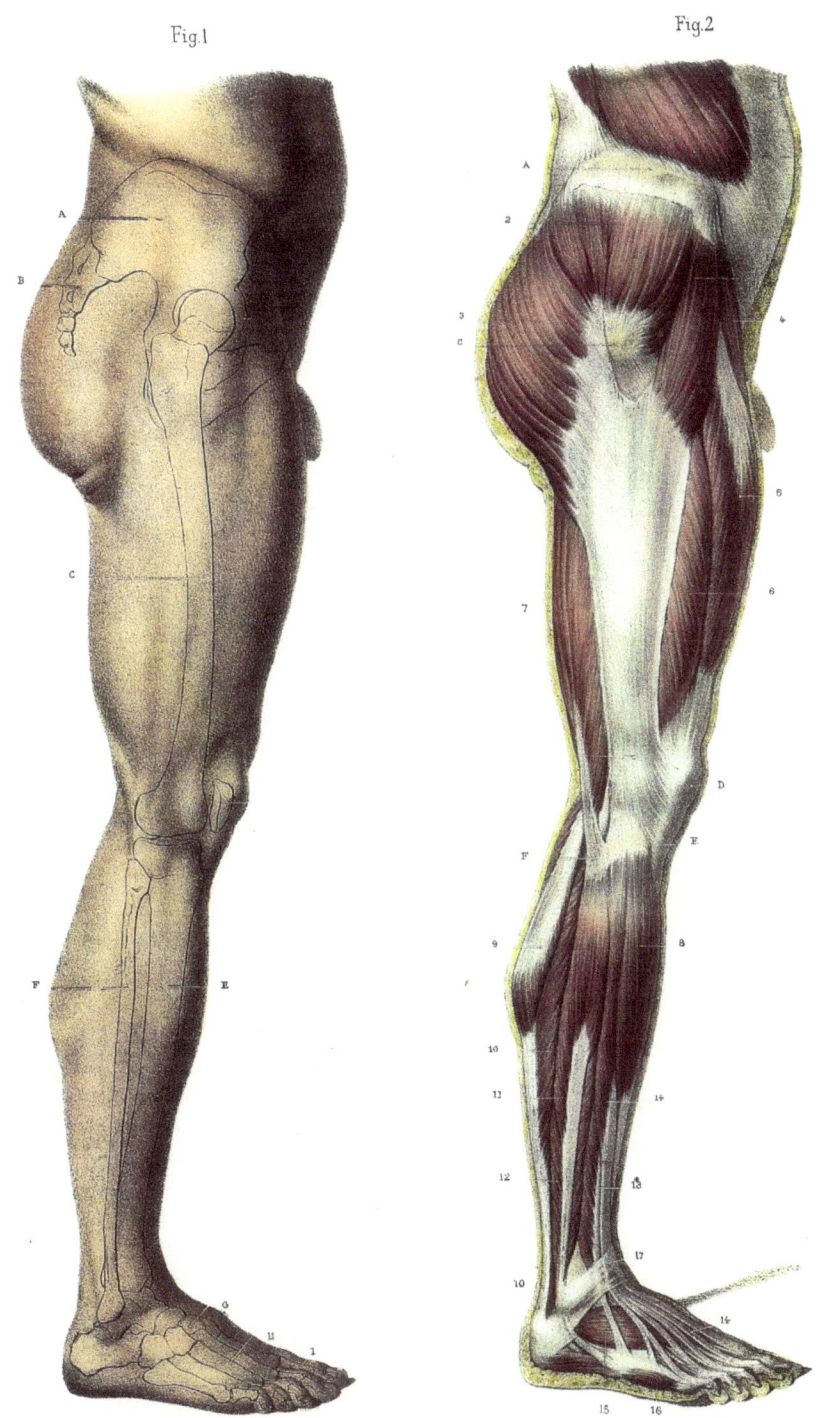

Fau. 2.ᵐᵉ edition   Paris   Imp Lemercier & Cᵉ. Paris
MÉQUIGNON MARVIS — GERMER-BAILLIÈRE

PLATE XXIII.

FIGURE 1.

A. Coxal bone.
B. Sacrum and coccyx.
C. Femur.
D. Rotula.
E. Tibia.
F. Fibula.
G. Tarsus.
H. Metatarsus.
I. Phalanges.

FIGURE 2.

A. Iliac crest.
C. Great trochanter.
D. Rotula.
E. External tuberosity of the tibia.
F. Head of the fibula.
 1. Tensor of the aponeurosis of the thigh.
 1'. Aponeurotic band.
 2. Gluteus medius.
 3. Gluteus maximus.
 4. Triceps.
 5. Biceps.
 6. Semi-tendinosus.
 7. Gastro-cnemii.
 8. Soleus muscle.
 9. Peroneus longus.
 10. Peroneus brevis.
 11. Long common extensor of the toes.
 11'. Tendons of this muscle.
 12. Anterior, or third peroneal muscle.
 13. Long extensor of the great toe.
 14. Tibialis anticus.
 15. Short common extensor of the toes.
 16. Abductor of the little toe.
 17. Annular ligament of the tarsus.

FIGURE 3.

A. Calcaneum.
B. Astragalus.
C. Scaphoid.
D. First cuneiform bone.
E. Second cuneiform.
F. Third cuneiform.
G. Cuboid.
H. Metatarsus.
I. Phalanges.

FIGURE 4.

A. Calcaneum.
 1. Short common flexor of the toes.

Attachments.—1°. To the calcaneum, and to plantar aponeurosis.
 2°. To the margins of the second phalanges of the four last toes.

 1'. Plantar aponeurosis, cut across.
 2. Abductor of the great toe. (*See* Pl. xx.)
 3. Short flexor muscle of the great toe.

Attachments.—1°. To the inferior surface of the calcaneum, and to the two last cuneiform bones.
 2°. To the metatarso-phalangean articulation of the great toe.

 4. Tendon of the long proper flexor of the great toe. (*See* Pl. xx.)
 5. Abductor of the little toe. (*See* Pl. xi.)
 6 and 7. Short floor of the little toe, and interosseal muscle.
 8. Lumbricales muscles.

71

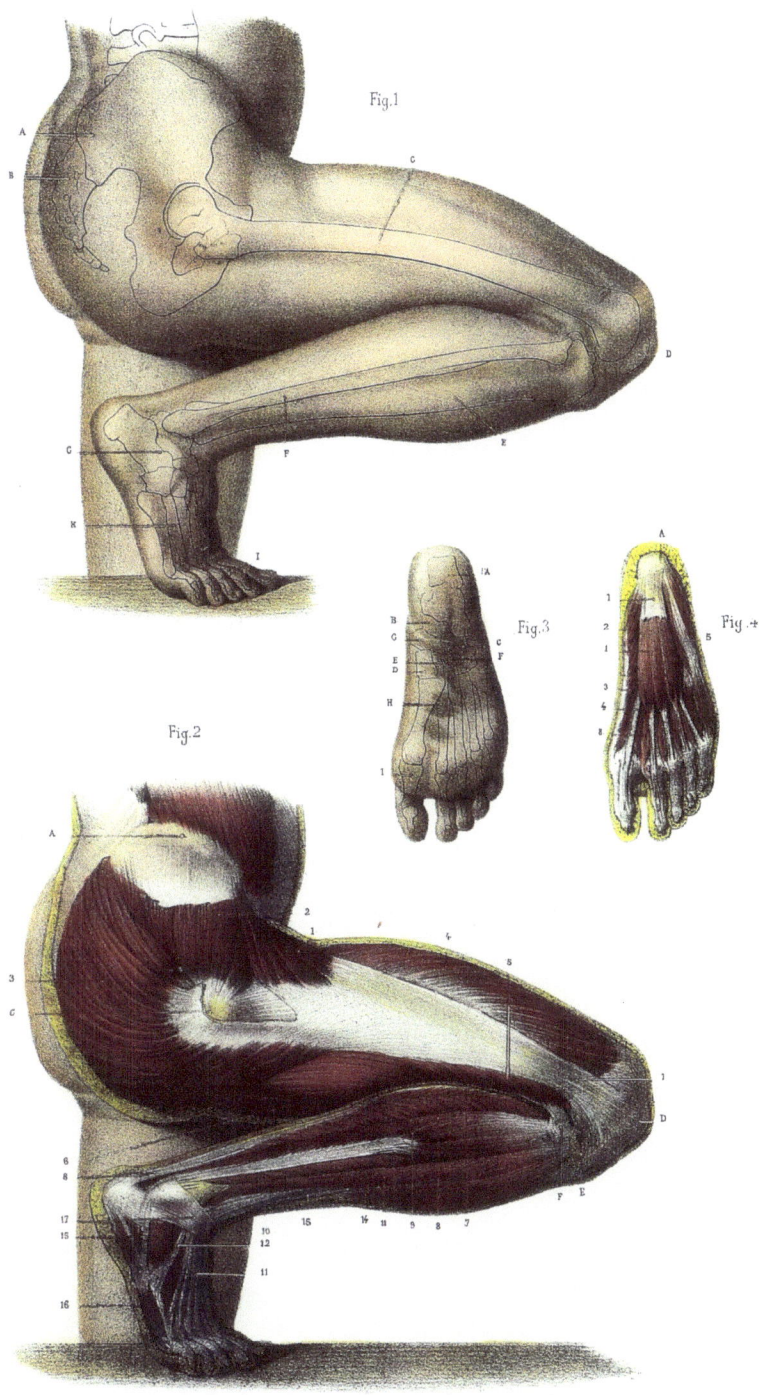

PL. 23

Fig.1

Fig.3

Fig.4

Fig.2

Paris

Imp Lemercier & Cᵉ Paris

MEQUIGNON MARVIS __ GERMER BAILLIÈRE

PLATE XXIV.

FIGURE 1.

A. A. Coxal bones.
B. Sacrum and coccyx.
C. Femur.
D. Rotula.
E. Tibia.
F. Perone.
G. Tarsus.
H. Metatarsus.
I. Phalanges.

FIGURE 2.

A. Anterior and superior iliac spine.
D. Rotula.
E. Tibia.
1. Rectus femoris.
2. Sartorius.
3. Psoas muscle.
4. Iliac muscle.
5. Pectineus.
6. First adductor muscle.
7. Gracilis muscle.
8. Third adductor muscle.
9. Semi-tendinosus muscle.
10. Triceps extensor muscle.
11. Gastro-cnemii muscles.
12 and 12'. Soleus and tendo-achilles.
13. Long common flexor of the toes.
14. Tibialis posticus muscle.
15. Tibialis anticus.
16. Adductor of the great toe.
17. Annular ligament of the tarsus.

FIGURE 3.

A. Tibia.
B. Fibula.
C. Astragalus.
D. Calcaneum.
E. Scaphoid.
F. First cuneiform bone.
G. Second cuneiform bone.
H. Third cuneiform bone.
I. Cuboid.
J. Metatarsus.
K. Phalanges.

FIGURE 4.

A. Malleolus internus.
B. Malleolus externus.
1. Annular ligament of the tarsus.
2. Tendons of the long common extensor of the toes.
3. Tendon of the long extensor of the great toe.
3. Tendon of the tibialis anticus.
5. Tendon of the anterior peroneus (peroneus tertius of Albinus).
6. Short common extensor of the toes.
7. Abductor of the little toe.
8. Adductor of the great toe.
9. Inter-osseal.
10. Anterior transverse metatarsal ligament.

73

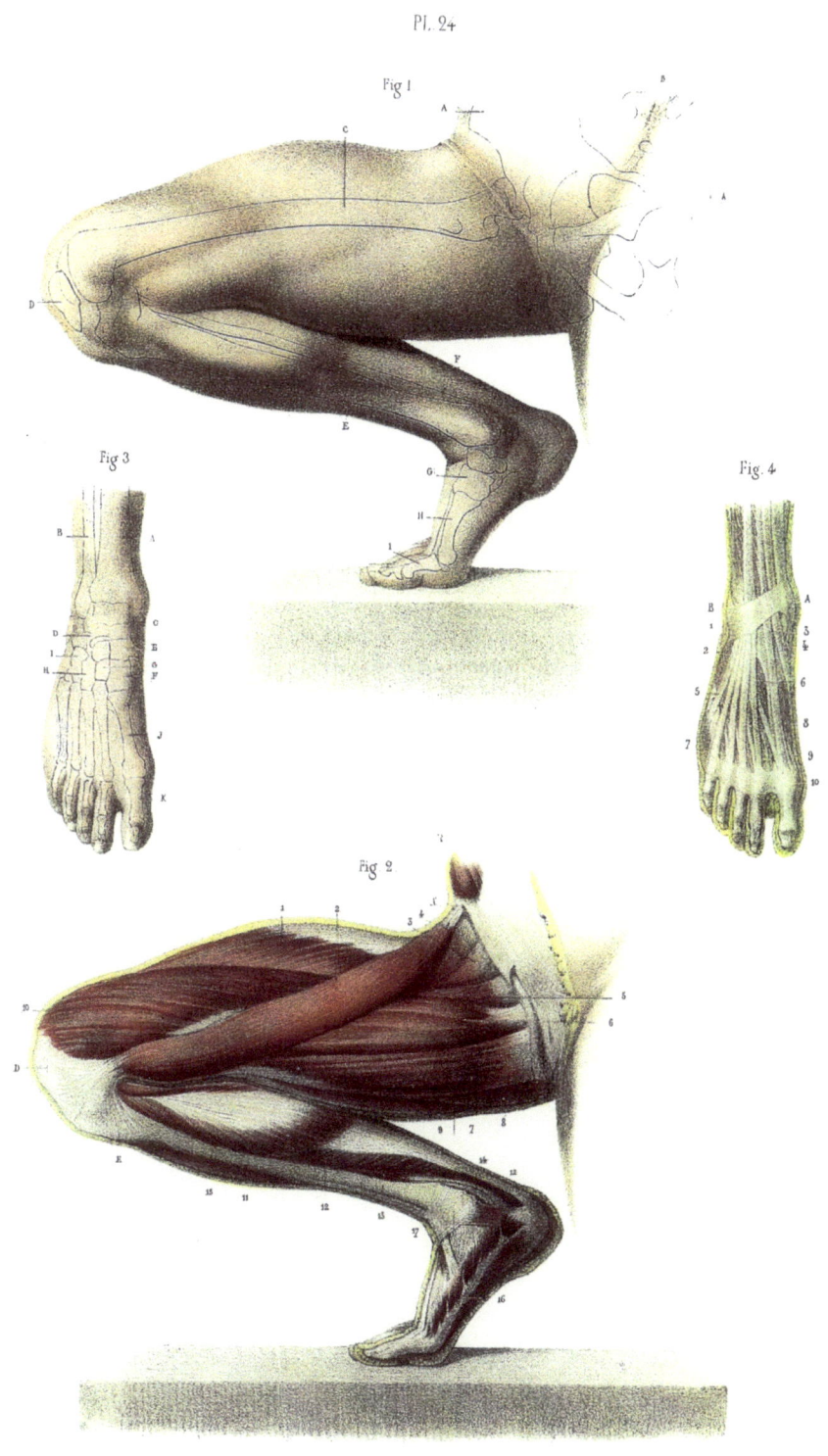

Pl. 24

Fig 1

Fig 3

Fig. 4

Fig 2

Pau 2me édition.   Paris   Imp. Lemercier & Cie Paris.
MÉQUIGNON MARVIS — GERMER BAILLERE.

PLATE XXV.

Dissection of the Laocoon, copied from the fine engraving of Bervie.

T. Pettitt & Co., Printers, Frith Street, Shaftesbury Avenue, W.

PL 25

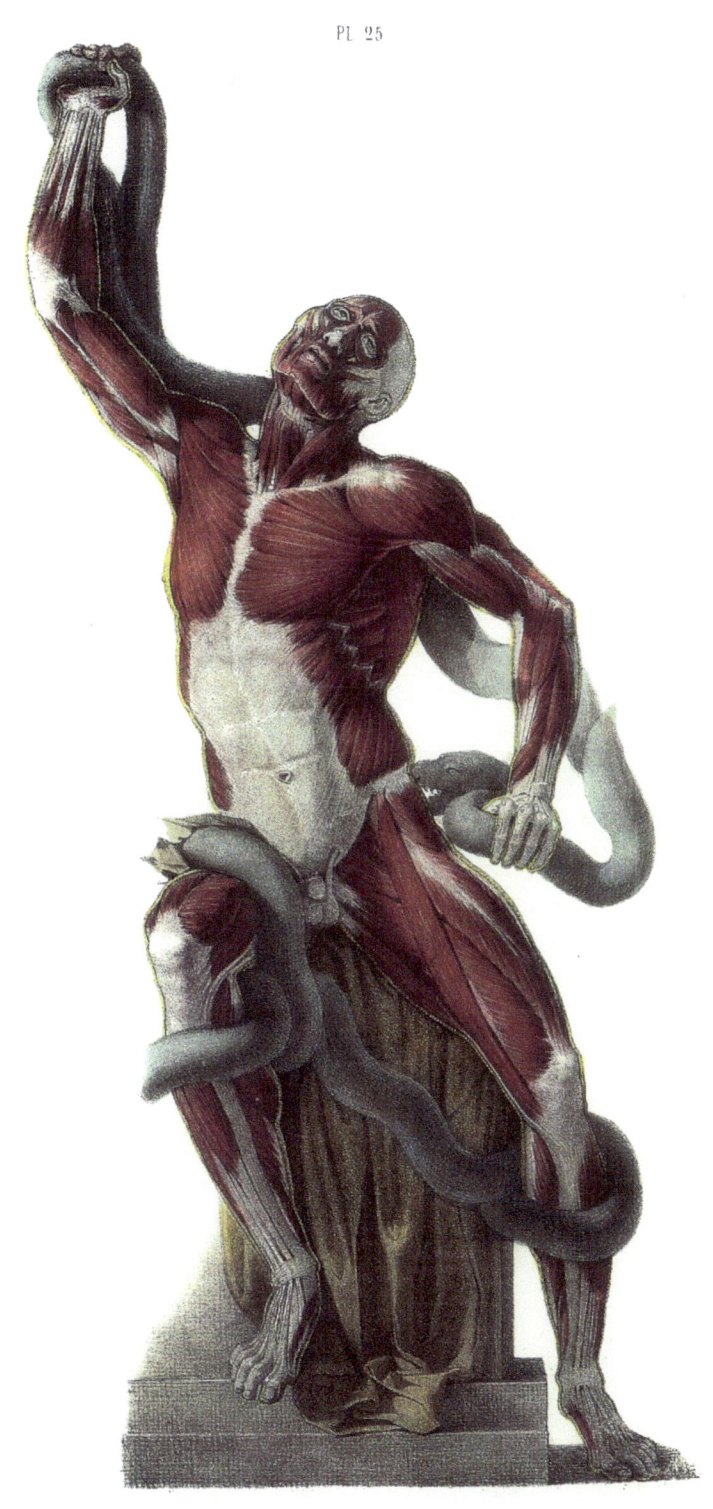

Fau 2me edition

Paris

Imp Lemercier Paris

MÉQUIGNON MARVIS   GERMER BAILLIÈRE

PLATE XXVI.

Dissection of the Gladiator.

T. Pettitt & Co., Printers, Frith Street, Shaftesbury Avenue, W.

PL.26.

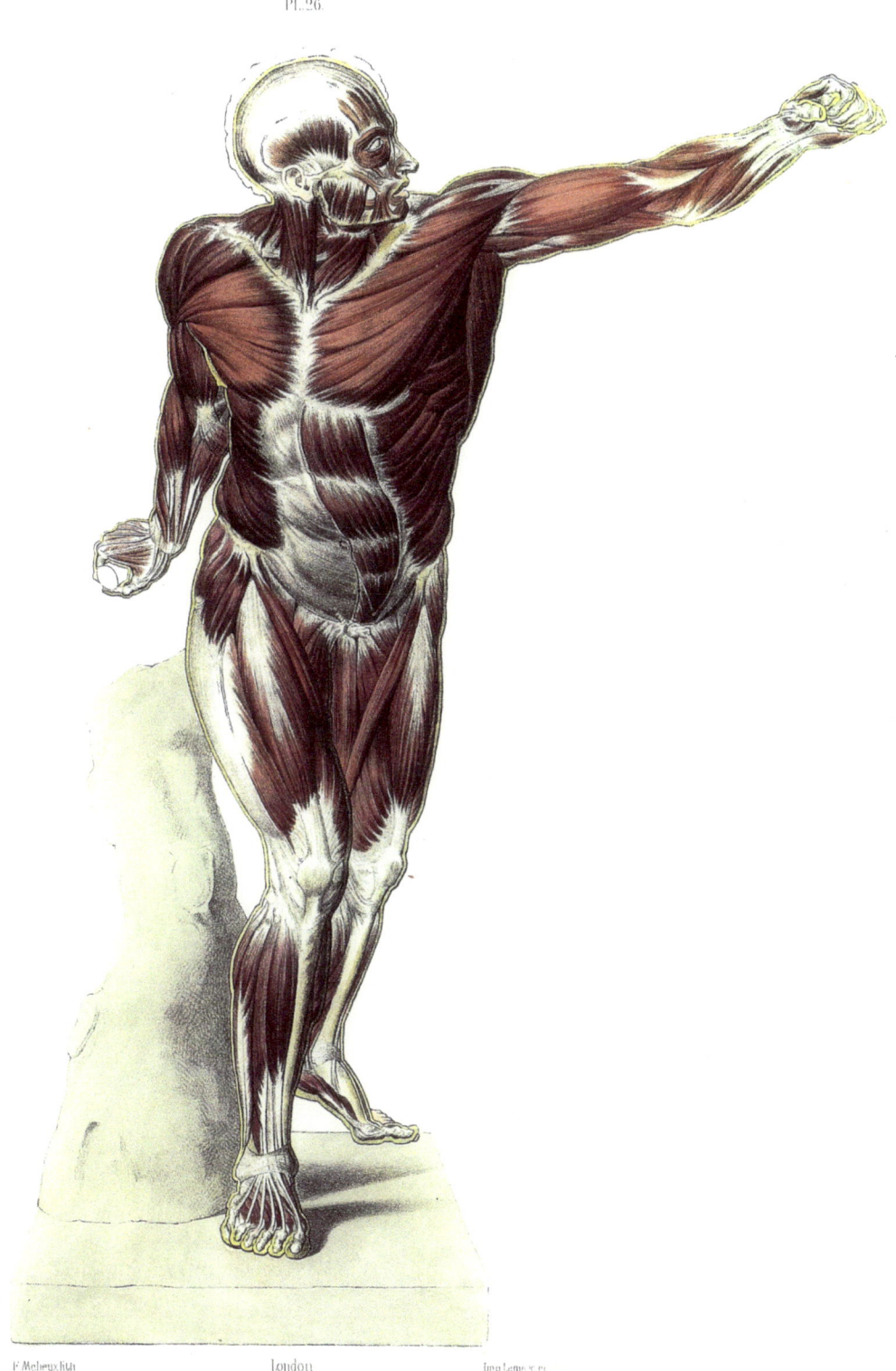

F. Meheuxthn.

London

Imp Lemer t rs

BAILLIÈRE, TINDALL & COX.

78

PLATE XXVII.

Dissection of Discobolus.

T. PETTITT & CO., PRINTERS, FRITH STREET, SHAFTESBURY AVENUE, W.

PL.27.

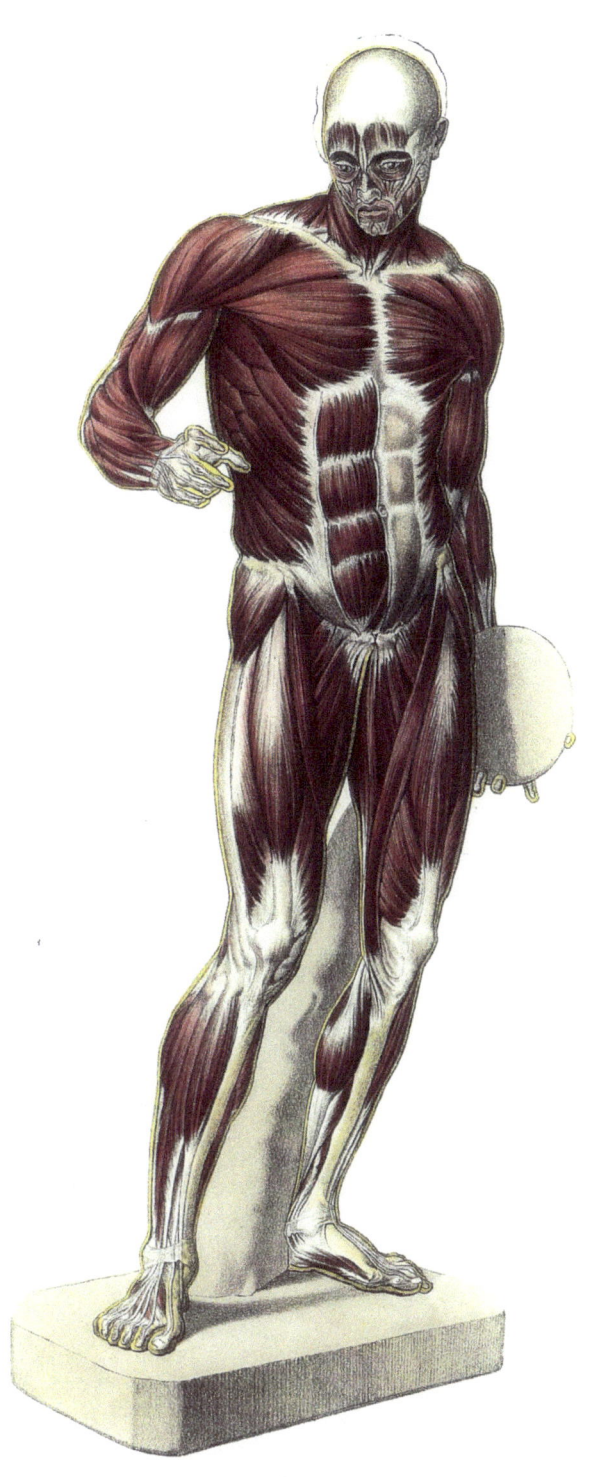

F.Meheux lith.

London

BAILLIÈRE, TINDALL & COX

Imp.Lemercier,Paris

Other Related Books:

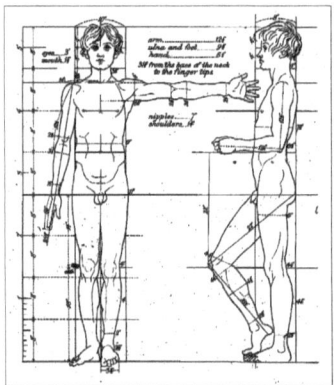

The Art Student's Guide
to the Proportions of the Human Form
By Dr. Johann Gottfried Schadow
edited by Tom Richardson
ISBN 978-0982167809

This is a republished edition of Dr. Schadow's famous work in which thirty plates demonstrate the proportions of the human form. It is based on the pioneering work of the Greek Sculptor Polycletus.

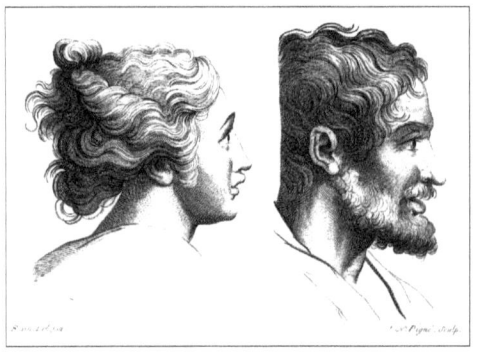

The School of Raphael
or the
Student's Guide to Expression in Historical Painting
by Louis Dorigny
described and explained by Benjamin Ralph
edited by Tom Richardson
ISBN 978-0982167849

These prints of the human head, showing the range of emotions and expressions, were engraved by the most skilled artists of the day from tracings and drawings made by Nicholas Dorigny from the famous cartoons that Raphael designed in the early 1500s to be made into tapestries for the Sistine Chapel. They were made into this book in 1859. Each plate has two versions, the first a fulley rendered, shaded print, the second an outline version, with dotted lines showing where highlights and shadows will be placed.

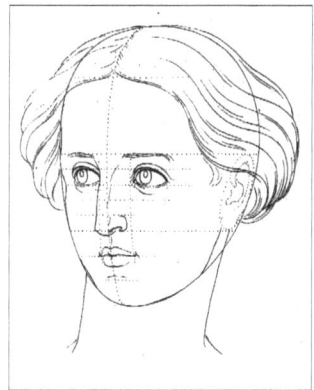

The Human Head
by Prof. Louis Bail
edited by Tom Richardson
ISBN 978-0982167830

How to draw the human head by the pre-eminent advocate for the teaching of drawing in schools in the mid nineteenth century, the inventor of the system of drawing used by many schools of the time.

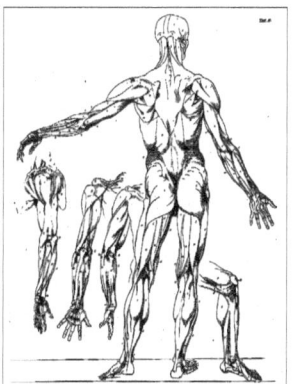

The Art Student's Guide
to the
Bones and Muscle of the Human Body:
and Lessons on Foreshortening
by Dr. Johann Gottfried Schadow
edited by Tom Richardson
ISBN 978-0982167823

This is a republished edition of Dr. Schadow's book which he designed for the benefit of his students at the Berlin Art Academy. It combines studies of anatomy based on his knowledge and the engravings of Bernhard Siegfried Albinus with three plates on human proportions plus detailed studies of the head tilted in different directions to demonstrate the effects of foreshortening.

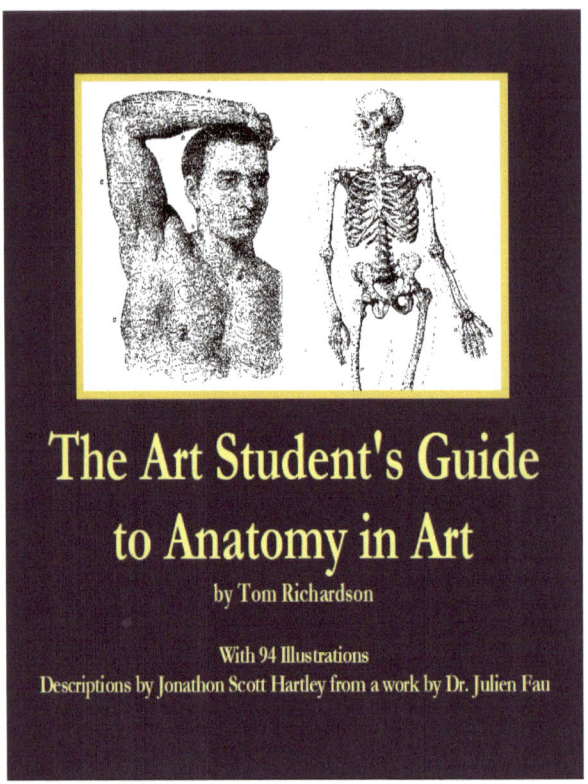

The Art Student's Guide to Anatomy in Art
by Tom Richardson

Descriptions by Jonathon Scott Hartley
Plates from a work by Dr. Julien Fau

ISBN 978-0982167861

This book is one of two that are based on the pioneering anatomical plates for art students first published by Doctor Julien Fau. This edition titled **The Art Student's Guide to Anatomy in Art** reproduces the black and white engravings and has a text written by Jonathon Scott Hartley in 1891 which combines an easy to understand description of the appearance and actions of the bones and muscles, with a concise description of the plates and has additional chapters on sculpting, muscles of the deeper layers, and human proportion.

www.ingramcontent.com/pod-product-compliance
Lightning Source LLC
Chambersburg PA
CBHW050736180526

45159CB00003B/1246